E

Dr. Pam Ross is by far one of the most positive and engaging voices of our time. Her grace and poise - coupled with her open and authentic presence emit a transforming influence on people of all ages.

In her compelling new book, Dr. Ross decodes the journey of success, in uncomplicated, yet deeply captivating language.

If you only plan to read one book this year, it has to be "Get Ready To Fly." I promise! You won't be disappointed.

Get ready to be inspired. Get ready to be enlightened. Get ready to Fly!

-Pastor Hart Ramsey
Founder, Northview Christian Church

Dr. Pam Ross's book "Get Ready to Fly, Preparing Your Soul to Soar" will have you ready to fly without a pilot's license. I read the book excerpts and was inspired and motivated to keep moving and soar even higher as it pertains to my God-given assignment.

Dr. Ross is so engaging, authentic, and smooth in her delivery of truth in this book. It inspires one to want to do more and then some.

-Veola Davis
Independent Mary Kay Sales Director

Life is a gradual and scalable journey, and it is so amazing how Dr. Pam uses very relatable aviation terminology to describe how we are expected to approach life, as well as live above clouds to get to where we are destined to arrive at.

From the realities of where you are coming from to the inevitable glitches we are met with along the way, as well as the possibilities of reaching where God has predestined us to get to. Dr. Pam did an excellent exposition to show us the possible successes of our lives without losing ourselves along the way.

This book is a must have and must hand-down even to coming generations. We all can fly but flying well is what's most profiting.

-Bidemi Mark-Mordi
Pastor, The Well Oasis Int'l and Life Coach

Pam is a master strategist with a wealth of knowledge and experience that shifts perspective, brings clarity, and pushes people into their greatness. Her care, personality, wit, and excellence is needed to healthily advance worlds. The context and content of this book are relevant, captivating, and easily applicable. We love the way Pam uses the flight metaphor to explore the steps needed to soar high and soar well!

-RAII & WHITNEY
Husband and Wife team.
Singers, Songwriters, Producers, and Coaches

Pam's commitment to excellence and wholeness is only surpassed by her commitment to God. She has a brilliant mind and a heart of gold. "Get Ready to Fly" is yet another extension of her natural passion, helping, and healing people. This book will take you on a journey that not only causes you to face your limitations but gives you the strategies to dismantle them.

-David S. Winston
Youth Pastor, Living Word Christian Center
Director, Bill Winston Ministries
Founder, Winston Leadership Institute

Dr. Pam's latest book "Get Ready To Fly" is a valuable prophetic resource for those that are serious about leaving their mark on the earth. I often say this about teaching, "If it's not practical, then it's not really spiritual". This book is crammed with useable information that you can use immediately!

As you read, "Get Ready To Fly", you will see yourself in its pages and locate where you are in your preparation process, in a measurable, practical way.

One side benefit of this book is that it will break off shame and fear; and stop gifted, qualified people from self-sabotaging themselves. I highly recommend both the book and Dr. Pam's team training skills.

-Prophet Kevin Leal

There is an unequivocal marriage between personal development and destiny attainment. The destination that you aspire to arrive at demands your development. Pam Ross has a transformative ability to help people, willing to learn, adjust their present for the safeguarding of their future. In her newest book, "Get Ready to Fly," she expertly empowers the reader to liberate themselves to soar into the future God designed for their life.

-Dr. Matthew L. Stevenson III
Global Senior Leader, The All Nations Collective

Dr. Pam Ross does it again in Get Ready to Fly! She's witty, brilliant and shares practical stories that hit home with powerful illustrations to shift hearts and mindsets!

She weaves a tapestry of excellence out of our everyday experiences that are relatable but deeply rooted in truth to free the soul to soar!

-Coach Anna McCoy
Anna McCoy Global Ventures, LLC

Dr. Pam Ross is one of the Kingdom's foremost life and leadership strategists. With over 20 years of executive experience in both Christian Ministry and Corporate Industry, she has divinely pencilled "Get Ready to Fly" to move you from a place of vision to strategy.

Dr. Pam Ross is gifted to mobilise manifestation, productivity and culture. With a heart to see fruitfulness in lives, leaders and organisations, she has brought together some of the richest truths on moving from your current place of purpose to your future place of destiny. Many times we know the end goal but lack the steps to manoeuvre and arrive. Dr. Pam Ross has carefully, practically and reasonably put together tools that all can engage with to forcefully lay hold of success.

Through this book, you will move from a place of latency to productivity, from a place of potential to fruitfulness, and from a place of stagnancy to success. I encourage you to engage this amazing and timely piece of wisdom for an abundant life.

-Elijah Israel Chanak
Founder, CEO & President,
Elijah Chanak International

Get Ready to Fly

Preparing Your Soul to Soar

Pam Ross

First Printing: 2020
ISBN 978-1-7325778-3-1

Printed in USA by Kingdom Leadership Development

Kingdom Leadership Development
2158 45th Avenue #148
Highland, IN 46322

Dedication

To Linda, for always believing I could fly!

"Hello Dr. Ross. Has your plane landed?

Table of Contents

SECTION FIVE
Tray Tables Up!

SECTION SIX
Silence Your Communication Devices

SECTION SEVEN
In Case of Loss of Cabin Pressure

Acknowledgements

A million thanks to our amazing flight crew! These people have been crucial in getting the principles of Get Ready to Fly in book form. A standing ovation goes to...

Air Navigator: Jenae McKnight for editing. Thank you for unlocking what I really know about elevation. Your guidance was invaluable.

Loadmaster: Deonna Adam for formatting. Thank you for being patient and knowledgeable. Can I write every book with you, please?

Flight Engineer: Lelita Pettigrew for believing there is nothing God said that "mama" can't do, with a team, a schedule and a deadline.

Flight Attendant: Diana Dumas for always serving up the "dope ish" and keeping my old self relevant.

Air Traffic Controllers:
Jessica Silas, for courageously declaring "This is a book."
Kelli Cossey for your consistent, "Go Apostle Go!

Foreword

The Metaphors from the Aviation Administration's Preflight Instructions is the perfect analogy to navigate our assignment.

Dr. Pam Ross, my sis, affectionately, is a powerful, practical, potential provoker. Her ability to rejuvenate a room with her glowing smile and fierce and tenacious approach to supporting the vision is unmatched. No one is better at tactfully caring for the individuals who are called to carry the mantle of a mission. Dr. Pam Ross is exceptional and an asset to anyone privileged to experience her. I've had that privilege for more than a decade and I am grateful for all she has poured.

This book is a much-needed manual for a missing ingredient in a very important conversation. Your gift can take you far, but it's your character that keeps you. Everybody will sell you strategies for successfully exercising your gift, but very few give you the secrets to securing your soul and developing your character while maintaining success. This practical guide is powerful if you are preparing to protect your promotion.

The process of purpose is intentional. Unfortunately, so many people want to skip the process. If we look from a Biblical lens we see nothing happens overnight. God protects his investment by developing people over time. Moses grew up in a system he was called to confront for 40 years. He spent 40 years in isolation before finding the proper instructions. After 80 years he was finally in position to free a nation of people.

Joseph had a dream that didn't come to pass for 13 years or so. He learned how to handle adversity and betrayal. His brothers threw him into a pit, but that pitting was really a planting that landed him in Potiphar's house. There his character was challenged. The experience ended up costing him his job but not his integrity. He was placed in prison where he found favor and sharpened his gift. It was necessary for him to go to prison to walk into his place of power—where his dream began.

David was separated from his family when God sent a prophet to anoint him. David's family never invited him to the party that was rightfully his. The oil wouldn't flow without him. Once he arrived he was anointed to be king. He spent almost 15 years going through various assignments and trials before he was king. He was submitted to and called to serve before ultimately replacing his successor, being seated in his assignment on the throne as long.

Even Jesus spent 30 years preparing for his assignment. What I am saying is that so many people want to show up in success but development is required and that takes time. There is preparation and process for your purposeful promotion.

This book reveals the power of preparation through relatable stories and real-life wisdom that Pam has earned through experience. Thank you, Dr. Pam Ross for this manual to achieve the mandate on our lives.

For every reader, get ready to soar.

Dr. Jermone Glenn

Introduction

"So, after this, I'm done!"

Linda just nodded her head, bit her lip, and kept driving. I was explaining to my dearest friend that she was driving me to my last and final ministry assignment. My family had just returned from a trip to Florida, where I had hoped some pressing issues would be addressed. They weren't. In fact, the dysfunction had been so strongly affirmed that I felt that my life would never change.

I had determined that if God wasn't going to intervene in my family life, I obviously wasn't fit for ministry. So, as Linda drove me to a hotel ballroom where I was to serve as the MC for a prophetic breakfast, I made plans for how we would spend our afternoon. Shopping, movies, or maybe even lunch. These breakfasts never served enough food for me. In retrospect, I was either pouting or punishing or both.

The prophetic breakfast was beautiful, and I was a graceful M.C. The time came for my final duty, introducing the keynote speaker. I read the prophet's biography and invited the crowd to welcome him with a standing ovation. As I surrendered the microphone and headed to my seat, my mind was on breakfast. Everyone else had been served, and I was scanning the room for the waiter to bring me a biscuit, a sausage, or something. This is probably why I didn't see the speaker take off walking around the perimeter of the entire ballroom, praying loudly in tongues. (Acts 2:4)

The Prophet made his way back to the front of the room, still praying on the microphone. As he approached my table, he said, "Pam, get ready to fly." I glanced up a little confused. "I see you surrounded by Louis Vuitton luggage." Now I was really confused. Not only had I quit ministry on the way there, I was financially broke. I was struggling to buy groceries, and this man was talking to me about a set of luxury luggage. It seemed unreal. "Oh, it's real," he said, "stand up!" I did.

"I see you getting on and off planes. I see you getting on and off your own plane. You're going to be in very high demand. I see you saying yes to pastors and leaders. You're going to help them operate in a spirit of excellence. Yes, I said a Spirit of Excellence." Now, this man had my full attention. I had recently committed to teaching a class titled "Developing a Spirit of Excellence" and had just started to build the curriculum.

At this time, I wasn't a consultant. I wasn't teaching or training anywhere other than my local church. I had no books, no blogs, no podcasts. No one knew my name, and I certainly wasn't getting on and off planes at anyone's request. It took all the faith I had to keep my minivan on the road. But somehow, a higher level of faith kicked in. I grabbed hold of that word, and I never let it go.

I printed a picture of a Louis Vuitton roller bag and framed it with the words, "Get Ready to Fly!" Suddenly, I went from quitting to being full of hope. I got excited when I imagined all the places I'd go and the people I would help. I kept that frame in my office at work and told the story to anyone who dared to ask me about it. I prayed and declared that word. As I began to travel and teach, I told every audience the story of the prophetic breakfast and the amazing word about flying. I would say, "We are standing in the dream of God!"

Several years later, I was asked to facilitate a development session for a group of leaders. As I prayed, I felt that their organization was entering into a season of elevation. I glanced at that framed word and decided to build the "Get Ready to Fly" training. The book you are holding is born from that training.

Now, here's the kicker! In all my excitement, I never realized that although prophetic, that word held instruction. God didn't just say, "Pam, you're going to fly." He said, "Get ready!" Here I am over twelve years on the other side of that prophetic breakfast. I've been on and off more planes than I can count. I have walked with God and endured many ups and several downs. I cannot honestly say I knew God was getting me ready to fly. I was just living my life, submitting to His will, and learning along the way.

It wasn't until I finished writing the manuscript that I realized how God had readied me for my elevation. He has delivered me from my fears. He has taught me how to be Pam Ross. He has stretched me to make hard decisions about what I really want in life. God has helped me to conquer my appetites. And probably the hardest part was getting control of my tongue. He has helped me recover from life's most challenging moments. I am overjoyed to share my wisdom and my research with you. What God has done for me -and is still doing for me- He will do for anyone who is willing to be made ready.

This book is about preparing your soul to soar. Together, we'll explore some strategies to prepare you for the success you've been working so hard to achieve. We'll use the Federal Aviation Administration's preflight instructions we are familiar with to guide us. We'll check your baggage; because we all have baggage. We'll help you take the right seat both spiritually and naturally and teach you how to courageously fasten your seatbelt. We'll understand the power of putting your tray table up because nothing tastes as good as a breakthrough. We'll silence your communication device and learn when to speak and when to just keep quiet. You will learn how to handle life's turbulence and hold on to only what's most important to you. And lastly, you'll get wisdom to properly respond to the unlikely and unexpected loss of cabin pressure.

Welcome aboard. I'm glad you're joining me on this journey. Get Ready to Fly!

You Don't Fly Drunk

LET'S BE FRANK

"I am not spending another night in the O'Hare Hilton, Frank!" Frank, who was obviously drunk, ignored his wife's vehement chastisement. "You're drunk, Frank!" she continued in a southern drawl that I would have found quite charming if she wasn't using it to publicly shame her husband. Frank or as she pronounced it, FRA-rank, appeared to have been, shall we say "over served" at one of the bars in Chicago O'Hare International Airport. He had staggered onto my 3-hour flight to California. He made his way down the aisle cheerfully greeting the other passengers as he steadied himself by grabbing the tops of their seats. With all eyes on him, Frank found and plopped down into his seat which was directly across the aisle from mine. "Oh goodie!" I thought. "This is going to be fun."

Frank seemed harmless enough to me. He appeared to be one of those "happy drunks" and I estimated he would be snoring loudly by the time we flew over the Rocky Mountains. Frank's wife, who had boarded before him, did not share my perspective. She raised her voice even louder, "Frank, you're drunk again!

Frank, I am sick of you! I am going to Hawaii with or without you, Frank!"

Suddenly and as if by magic, four, yes FOUR, sky marshals appeared. "They are coming for you, Frank!" His wife announced in one of those I-told-you-so type of ways. She was right. These four men escorted friendly Frank and his worried wife off of our plane without saying one word.

It was on that flight that I learned most airlines have a hard and fast rule. You don't fly drunk!

According to medical research, alcohol affects you differently in the air. It has something to do with the barometric pressure. So even though Frank was friendly on the ground, there was no way to predict his demeanor at 10,000 feet. Frank was not allowed to fly. But it wasn't because of his current state. His denial was because of what was in him. That was the day I learned that elevation causes what's in your belly to quickly go to your head. A manager with a leading airline company once told me "A gate agent can cancel a passenger's reservation if he or she even smells drunk!" They are just too unpredictable in the air.

The ability of sudden elevation to alter your internal state is not just true on airplanes. It's true in all of our lives. We've heard more than a few tragic stories of "death by success." Athletes who finally go pro, only to lose it all to drug addiction. Musicians who make it to the top of the industry and leave us all too soon, choosing suicide to escape the pressures of fandom. Actors who are more known for their time in rehab than their roles in television and film. Politicians who honorably served their local community but left a legacy of scandal to the global community. Marriages held together by the struggle, strangely fizzled out when their ship finally came in. I'm sure you can name at least one person in your world who crashed and burned under the pressure caused by sudden elevation. Some of us are those people!

Power and Money

It's been said that power and money don't change you, they only reveal you. The higher you go the more people will see you and have something to say about what your success reveals. I'm not talking about dark family secrets, the proverbial skeletons in the closet or anything external for that matter. I am certainly not advocating living your life in fear of what "they" might say. As we level up in life, we leave our past behind. The deadliest weapons, the ones most likely to cause a crash landing, are the self-destructing weapons inside of our own souls. Sometimes we won't know what's in us until the power is plugged in.

In my work roles, I am both a second-chair leader and a CEO. Most of what I make happen is by delegated authority. I've seen first-hand what happens when gifted people are given too much power too soon. Let's just say authority is like a stiff drink and not everyone can hold their liquor. Some get drunk with power and like Frank, they've been escorted off my team. Over the years, I've learned to delegate power and authority in small sips rather than big gulps. Because no matter how sweet someone appears on the outside, not even they know how they will respond when faced with sudden freedom.

I saw a terrible prank on YouTube. A group of guys recorded the lottery drawing on the news. Then they purchased a ticket with those same numbers. The next night they played the recording as if it was live and tricked their friend into believing he had finally won the lottery for millions of dollars. The joke turned on them when this poor guy jumped to his feet and told each and every one of his friends what he really felt about them. He held nothing back! He emptied his whole heart! And it was nothing they wanted to hear. Just imagine him jumping from the couch and one by one facing each of them. "I never liked you!" "You're a loser!" "You're an idiot!"

I thought the video was hilarious, but as I think back on it, these guys were clearly hurt and heartbroken. I wonder if their friendship ever recovered. The video does prove my point, because this man didn't change in an instant. He didn't even have the money yet, so wealth couldn't possibly have changed him. The very thought of those millions of dollars made him feel free to reveal what was already in his heart.

Money doesn't change you, it reveals you.

I'm not downing success. We all love a good come-up story. But coming up involves a change in both internal and external atmospheric pressure and not everyone is prepared to handle it. In today's rise and grind world, everybody wants to be a star. And with the use of social media, everybody can be. Gone are the days of waiting to be discovered. Our futures are in our own hands now. We can upload YouTube videos, launch podcasts, go live on Facebook and Instagram to an immediate global audience. In my writing career, I received one rejection letter and decided to self-publish. Who wants to wait? There is money to be made and fame to be had. But how do we ensure the success we're building won't be the worst thing that ever happened to us or our families?

"I don't know what they want from me. It's like the more money we come across, the more problems we see."

As a personal development coach, I help clients navigate their way to the goals they set. It's my responsibility to help these leaders lift their dreams off the ground and soar. I am also a pastor. I have the privilege of providing guidance and counseling to people who are navigating the stresses of life. Many of those stresses are caused by the things we work hard for, even pray for, things like marriage, children, promotion, opportunity and money. It didn't take long for me to start seeing a pattern. We work hard to achieve new levels of success. New levels of success reveal insecurity, trigger trauma or activate the imposter syndrome. I was working both ends of the cycle and there had to be a more efficient way to help people.

Avoiding success is not the way to avoid pressure. Untapped potential can make you miserable and haunt you to death. Don't put yourself in bondage to fear by attempting to avoid the stress of success. As my best friend, Linda says, "I've been bound, and I've been free. Free is better." Furthermore, the whole world suffers when we fail or refuse to fulfill our purpose. Don't forfeit your win because of what comes with it.

"I've been bound, and I've been free. Free is better!"
Minister Linda Cobb

I'm the Greatest!

Jesus is my personal hero. I endeavor to live and lead by the principles He taught. One day He was walking with his team of twelve young men and overheard them arguing about who would be the greatest in His Kingdom. Allow me to insert this fact about me. At the time of this writing, I work in an office with thirteen young men. (There are only four other women in the building) I am 15 years older than the oldest of the guys. To say I am getting an education about the world of young men would be an understatement. Each of them is gifted, powerful and extremely bright. They have a brotherhood that I enjoy observing. They are princely, yet comical, spiritual and yet so very real with each other. Using my work life, I can imagine the many road trips Jesus took with His team of twelve. I can imagine them having a heated argument complete with supporting evidence about who will be the greatest in the Kingdom of Heaven.

Jesus never told any of His disciples not to desire greatness. He never accused them of being selfish or full of empty ambition. Instead, He told them how to achieve greatness. In His Kingdom the greatest is the one who serves others. (See Matthew 23:11) Jesus' leadership tactic was to instruct and it is mine as well. Like those early followers of Jesus, I want to be great. I want my life to impact the world around me. Like you, I want to walk in my divine purpose. I want to fulfill my destiny, and I want to do it all while living in my true identity. But I don't want to lose myself along the way.

The Bible recounts the story of the migration of the Jewish people from slavery in Egypt to the land God promised their forefather, Abraham. These people had endured all the atrocities associated with slavery for over 400 years. To say they were ready to walk in their promise was an understatement. But instead of taking them directly to the place of promise, God took them on the scenic route through years of wilderness living. How horrible!! I would have wanted to go to my promise, go directly to my promise, "do not pass go, do not collect two hundred dollars." But God explains the necessity of the long route.

> *And you shall remember [always] all the ways which the Lord your God has led you these forty years in the wilderness, so that He might humble you and test you, to know what was in your heart (mind), whether you would keep His commandments or not. 3 He humbled you and allowed you to be hungry*

and fed you with manna, [a substance] which you did not know, nor did your fathers know, so that He might make you understand [by personal experience] that man does not live by bread alone, but man lives by every word that proceeds out of the mouth of the Lord. Deuteronomy 8:2 AMP

I am convinced that the lessons we learn on our way to success are what sustain us in success. Growing pains lead to supporting wisdom. There are lessons to be learned in the wilderness. Humility is agreeing with what God says about you. It's the journey that prepares us to live in the promise.

However, because today's path to success is shorter, faster and more visible we need to be intentional about our preparation. Otherwise, we will arrive at the place of success and stand in the spotlight naked. We will get what you've hoped for, prayed for and worked for only to break under the weight of our own productivity.

Check Your Baggage

OVERLOADED

Aliyah Dana Haughton, an American singer and actress, was killed in a plane crash on August 25, 2001, at the Marsh Harbour Airport on the Abaco Islands, Bahamas. She had just completed filming for the music video for her single "Rock the Boat." Employees of Virgin Records America accompanied her on the flight. The Cessna 402 twin-engine light aircraft, registered to Skystream Inc. and operated by Blackhawk International Airways Inc. was piloted by Luis Morales III and crashed shortly after takeoff.[1] In addition to Aaliyah, eight people were killed in the plane crash. She was 22 years old.

Here's the back story.

The passengers had grown impatient because the Cessna was supposed to arrive at 4:30 p.m. EDT, but did not arrive until 6:15 p.m. EDT.[3] Charter pilot Lewis Key claimed to have overheard passengers arguing with the pilot, Luis Morales III, prior to take off, adding that Morales warned them that there was too much weight for a "safe flight". Key further stated: "He tried to convince them the plane was overloaded, but they insisted they had chartered the plane and they had to be in Miami Saturday night."[9] Key indicated that Morales gave in to the passengers and that he had trouble starting one of the engines.[10]

The death of R&B super star Aliyah brought heartbreak to her fans and a tremendous loss to the music industry.

"These people didn't need to die," said Eddie Golson, the owner of Pro-Freight Cargo Service, which handled the cargo shipments for the video in the Bahamas. "This all could have been avoided if they had just followed the rules."

Sadly, it's easy to blame the pilot or the passengers for this tragedy. However, I can relate to the decisions made that day. If you've ever taken what seemed at the time to be a small risk, you should relate too. Have you ever texted while driving or ridden in the car with a buzzed driver? Have you ever had unprotected sex with someone without having "the talk"? Heck, have you ever eaten a coworker's lunch from the breakroom refrigerator? These are all things that are potentially harmful or deadly. We know we shouldn't do them and yet we do them! "Just this once" we say to ourselves, "after all, what are the odds." The aviation rules and guidelines are established to lower or eliminate the odds of harm or death. There are forces actively working against the guidelines and rules. Forces inside of us.

I can imagine these passengers were impatient. Afterall, the plane was expected to arrive at 4:30 p.m. and didn't arrive until 6:15 p.m. That's one hundred

and five minutes of waiting, for people who, I'm speculating here, generally didn't have to wait for what they wanted. When you've waited for something for a long time and it finally looks like it's happening, you want it to happen now! If you don't believe me, ask any newlywed. Impatience can cause you to cut corners and overlook wisdom especially when you've waited longer than expected and it feels like things are finally about to take off for you.

They had finished their work. I travel for work quite often. When I arrive, I'm energized and excited about what is about to happen. Although I'm social by nature, before my presentation, training or consultation, I'm not very chatty. My focus is on the work I'm there to do. This is a stark contrast to my demeanor after the work is done, I get a little loopy and I can be very "lax" in the definitive sense. I'm less strict and less observant. After my work, I have forgotten books in Georgia, glasses in Colorado, even my cellphone in Pennsylvania. I am writing this fresh from a trip where I left my winter coat in my hotel room! Thankfully, I remembered and was able to get a new key, go back up and get it. Success often happens after doing the hard work or passing the hard tests. In fact, it's the work and the tests that put that success in motion. When the "hard part" is done, you're more likely to ignore details and bypass your intuition.

Another reason I can relate to this crash is the flight was short and appeared easy. Overloading a ninety-minute flight doesn't seem as dangerous as overloading a long one. That's a deceptive notion, because flight has nothing to do with distance. It's all about speed and lift. The aircraft crashed shortly after takeoff, about 200 feet (60 m) from the runway. Research shows that most car accidents happen within five minutes or less of the driver's home. Even more shocking is the most common type of collision is drivers hitting parked cars! When you're so close to where you are headed, there is a comfort zone effect, muscle memory kicks in and drivers are less alert. The same is true for soaring in life. When things are so close to taking off for you, it's not the time to ease up.

This is the time to maintain your standards, stay alert and push through until take off.

This overloaded plane reminds me of some overloaded lives I've seen both in ministry and in coaching. Susan, (not her real name) felt as if her dreams were right at her fingertips, but she just couldn't get her life moving forward and her dreams off the ground. She lacked energy and focus. When she tried to launch her ideas, they seemed to lift off and then would crash around her, leaving her emotionally and financially devastated. Although she knew she was destined for more, she just couldn't develop hope. When she had decided she could no longer tolerate this low-level life, she contacted me for coaching. We met and what we discovered was a life weighed down by trauma.

"Tell me about the worst thing that ever happened to you." My strategy was to get Susan to recognize that even though this "worst thing" happened to her, she was still alive. She survived it and there's victory in that. I wanted to springboard off of her answer and renew her faith in herself. But our session took a different turn. Susan told me about a medical emergency that seemed to her to come out of nowhere. She had emergency surgery that left her infertile. Infertility is a form of trauma.

I sensed an opening there and together, we stepped into it. I asked some hard questions and she courageously answered. "How did you see yourself after this incident?" "How did you see God?" "How did you see the world?" You see, trauma is a teacher. It tells us stories as a coping mechanism for the things we can't control or don't want to face. As we go through life, trauma happens to all of us. If we are not careful, we will live our lives according to the lessons taught by trauma rather than by the truth.

> *"Sanctify them by the truth, your word is truth." John 17:17 NIV*

Susan did the work to unpack some heavy emotions. She recognized altered perceptions of herself caused by trauma. She unpacked guilt, unforgiveness, shame, victimization and so much more. She began to embrace her true identity and exercise her true power. In a matter of days, her life became lighter. Today, she is full of hope, executing vision and is moving forward with her life. She is living free and ready to soar.

When I talk to congregants or clients about living free, I am referring to living a life free from the things that weigh our souls down. These are things we pick up and pack up from trauma, things inherited from our DNA or family history. These things make lift off difficult, flying dangerous and crashing inevitable. In order to have a safe flight to your dream life, your destination, it's important to allow your heart, your mind and your desires to be inspected before takeoff. We have to be willing to divorce ourselves from low-level living and thinking regardless of where those habits or mindsets originated. A more experienced counselor once told me "Regardless of what or who caused the pain, it's the client's responsibility to get healed." Like my coaching client, Susan discovered, even if you didn't cause the hurt, you have to cause the healing!

Here's great news! If God is pressing on your life for healing and wholeness, it is an indication that your life is about to be elevated. Moses had to take off his shoes before he received his instructions from God to deliver a nation. (Exodus 3:5) Jacob wrestled with God all night before he changed his name to Israel and destined him to be the progenitor of a chosen people. (Gen 32:28) Esther was purified and beautified for 12 months before she was crowned queen and through her graciousness, preserved a people. (Esther 2:12) After Apostle Paul was called, he spent years in Arabia beginning his ministry that brought the Gospel to the Gentiles. (Galatians 1:17) And the Greatest of all time, Jesus, was baptized to fulfill all righteousness and was then led into the desert for 40 days before He introduced the Kingdom of Heaven and became Savior of the World. God required a process for each of these great people and He will require a process of your great self.

A little over two months after the September 11th terrorist attack, the United States established the Transportation Security Agency, TSA. It is the TSA that determines what is and what is not allowed on an airplane. It is the TSA that, unless you are granted precheck status, requires you to remove your computer, take off your shoes, coats and belts. It is the TSA that requires you to part from your beloved cell phone, pass through metal detectors, x-ray machines, be subjected to pat-downs and discretionary searches.

Just like the TSA sets mandates on our luggage for our safe travel to our destination, God makes these requirements for our safe arrival to destiny. They can be painful, and they can be uncomfortable, but the requirements of God reflect His love for us and they are for our good. It is the only way to empty our powder keg.

Empty the Powder Keg

I have a theory that may help you understand the love involved in the requirements of God. Imagine your weaknesses, brokenness and character flaws are the gun powder in a powder keg. (A powder keg is a barrel of gun powder. It has become a metaphor for a dangerous or volatile situation.) Now imagine that you carry that powder keg under your left arm everywhere you go. The keg may be hidden but it is, nevertheless, very explosive and dangerous to you and those around you. Here's my theory. The enemy of your soul will not explode the gun powder while you're on the ground. He will wait until you have some measure of success, some level of elevation and then create the right flame to cause your brokenness to destroy your life. This is why the purposes of God for your life require an examination and removal of anything that would keep you from becoming the prevailing person He created you to be. This is not about religious rules. This is about living powerful and free! There's a passage in the Bible that gives a rundown of some things that will keep us out of the free life.

It is obvious what kind of life develops out of trying to get your own way all the time: repetitive, loveless, cheap sex; a stinking accumulation of mental and emotional garbage; frenzied and joyless grabs for happiness; trinket gods; magic-show religion; paranoid loneliness; cutthroat competition; all-consuming-yet-never-satisfied wants; a brutal temper; an impotence to love or be loved; divided homes and divided lives; small-minded and lopsided pursuits; the vicious habit of depersonalizing everyone into a rival; uncontrolled and uncontrollable addictions; ugly parodies of community. I could go on.

> *This isn't the first time I have warned you, you know. If you use your freedom this way, you will not inherit God's kingdom. Galatians 5:19-21 Message Bible*

Check out this list derived from the above scripture. Notice how these weights may appear now and at the next level of influence and exposure. If you're feeling pressure to address any of these issues in your life, the good news is, you're getting ready to fly. It's time to prepare your soul to soar.

Pre-flight check list.

	How this looks on the ground	How this looks in the air
Sexual impurity	The inability or refusal to control sexual appetites, promiscuity, pornography, lewd thoughts or actions	The use or abuse of yourself or others for pleasure, reward or stress relief. Cruelty, apathy, lying, rape
Idolatry and sorcery	Stubbornness and closed-mindedness. The attempt or desire to control the minds, feelings or desires of others, codependency, people pleasing	Recreating the "truth" to forward a personal agenda, mind control, god complex, poverty, insanity
Hatred and contentions	Unforgiveness, insistence on receiving an apology, quick to speak, slow to hear, judgmental, argumentative	Isolation, loneliness, bitterness, unresolved sicknesses

Jealousies; outbursts of wrath	Compulsive comparison to others. Uncontrolled emotions, unpredictable actions, moodiness	Surrounded by 'yes men" Refusal to take ownership of mistakes. Irrelevancy, delusional, paranoid
Selfish ambitions, dissensions	Rebellion against authority, bullying, pride, dishonor	Overt racism, gender bias, intolerance, extortion, betrayal, bribery, destruction, death
Heresies	Manipulation, guilt-trips, condemnation, false humility, legalistic	Destruction, greed, extortion, strife, wickedness, thievery, emotional abuse, insanity
Envy and murders	Wanting what others have, rather than one's own. Participating in scandal, rumors, gossip or character assassinations	Cruelty, misappropriation, fraud, plagiarism, discontentment, murder

Drunkenness and revelries	Lack of boundaries, avoidance of hard things or hard truths, escapism, victimization,	irresponsibility, blaming, recklessness, addictions, lasciviousness, suicide

Many years ago, I was working on an annual women's conference and something happened that really wounded me. I was at work and a gentleman approached me saying, "Hey, can men come to the women's conference? I may have to come to this one!" He showed me an advertisement for the conference to be held in the fall. Imagine my shock when I saw my face and name among the speakers! No one had said anything to me about it, but I chalked it up to an oversight. I started thinking about how historic it would be for me, a Black woman, to be a featured speaker at this event.

Planning for the conference progressed over the weeks and months and people began to get excited about Pam Ross speaking at this event. My likeness was included in the video and print advertisement and people were signing up by the hundreds. I will admit, it was exciting! Eventually people began to ask about the event schedule, specifically, when was Pam speaking? Although the schedule was never officially released to registrants, someone accidentally leaked it to the staff. My name wasn't on it. I was never scheduled to speak. I was caught between a rock, (recognizing that I had you've been used,) and a hard place, (deciding if I would play along or tell the truth.) Truth won.

When people asked me when I was speaking, I said "Oh, I'll be here." or "I can't really say." Eventually the truth came out that Pam Ross was not going to be a speaker. Rumors spread. The results were devastating. Over nine hundred women had registered. However, on opening night, less than ninety showed up. Imagine preparing for nearly a thousand people and looking out and seeing under one hundred. My leaders were horribly embarrassed in front of their guests. They were understandably angry and I was the convenient scapegoat.

I endured a betrayal and accusation followed by an extended character assassination. It was such a painful season that I prayed, "God if this event is not in your will, shut it down because it's a weapon in the hands of my enemy." The Lord shut the women's ministry down and that conference was not held again for five years.

As God was bringing me out of that place and elevating me to the next, there was talk of reviving this same woman's ministry. When I first got wind of it, I thought to myself, this thing will not come back; it cannot be reconstructed. But the Lord said, "It's going to happen and you're going to make it happen." Sure enough, I was directed to rebuild it from the ground up. I organized a team of 125 women. I was successful, but I had a very bad attitude. I didn't understand why, as I was leaving this place, was I having to rebuild something that had been so painful to me. I had told a lot of people I was leaving that year. I had prepared in every way I knew how, and no new opportunities had opened up for me. Finally, here we are in November and not only was I still there, I was rebuilding the thing that had caused me pain. One day, as I pulled up to the building, I got out of my car and the Lord said, "I want you to build this like you're building it for you. I want you to make sure everything is done right and make it beautiful."

That's when the light bulb in my head came on! God wanted me to unpack pain and resentment so I could be elevated out of there. This was the final test! He was checking my baggage. God did not want the pain of rejection to go with me and turn into trust issues and rebellion against leaders in my future. My entire attitude changed! I did what was needed to ensure this event would be beautiful and come off without a hitch.

As I woke up the day before the conference, the Lord said to my heart, "You're going to serve them Sunday." After waiting almost a year, I was finally released!!! I submitted my notice of resignation and it was received honorably.

But here's the interesting part. Nearly a year later a former coworker called me. He had been hired by an internationally-known ministry with locations in three states. This ministry was hosting its first conference for women and wanted him to organize it. He called me because he had seen my work at my previous place of employment. I sent him all of my "How to" plans and he organized a great event. The following year, the same gentleman called again. This time, his boss was looking for a speaker, someone who had lived through divorce and regained her joy! Remarkably, I had just released the book, The Force of Joy, building an unstoppable you. I was invited to be a speaker at one of the fastest-growing events for women in the world. Friends and colleagues asked me how on earth did I get this coveted opportunity. I couldn't explain it and they wouldn't have believed me.

The host of this conference, the big one, the international one, the famous one, was the keynote speaker of the conference I was asked to rebuild just two years prior. Although I organized it, we never met. Only God can make something like this happen. I thank God I didn't become one of those women leaders who doesn't' like women's events or women for that matter. All I can say is "I'm so glad I checked my bags!

The Naked Emperor

It's important to allow the Lord to deal with our character before we level up, because as we rise in success, there will be fewer voices who will. There is a children's story about an emperor who was tricked by charlatans into purchasing imaginary garments. These thieves told the Emperor that only the wisest and most cultured people could detect the special fabric they wove. After paying a very high price for these clothes, the Emperor got "dressed" and paraded through the town stark naked!! The townspeople all pretended they could see magnificent clothing. But a little child yelled from the crowd "The Emperor is naked!"

As you elevate, both your ability to do good for people and your ability to do bad to people increases. Unfortunately, this means that you will have less access to the truth about yourself. Have you ever seen successful people do crazy things with a whole entourage to support them? That's because no one wants to tell powerful people things they don't want to hear. This could work to your disadvantage if you happen to be the powerful one.

Checking your baggage allows you to be a leader who can handle the truth about your organization and about you. If you're a loaded powder keg, no one wants to be the one to set you off. You could live in a false reality, surrounded by handlers and not helpers and putting yourself and everyone else in danger of crashing and burning. Being emotionally balanced, or can I say balancing your emotional baggage, makes you approachable and reasonable. You will be less likely to be manipulated like the naked emperor. You will live in a healthy environment with real relationships.

All right, now that your baggage is at a healthy weight, welcome aboard, you need to find the right seat.

Take the Right Seat

LOCATION, LOCATION, LOCATION

Ma'am, is your name, James Allenson? I sheepishly looked at the flight attendant and said, "No, it's not. Do I need to move?" "Oh, no." She said, "Just making sure he's not here. You can have his seat."

My teammate, James was scheduled to join me on a church consultation in Charlotte, North Carolina. We needed to make a last-minute personnel change and found that purchasing a round-trip ticket for someone else was less than the cost of changing the ticket. So, when the gate attendant announced, "Ladies and gentlemen, this is a full flight." I had a great hope I'd have an empty seat next to me. It turns out I was right. The assumption was James had missed his flight when actually, he never showed up for it.

As the plane took off without James, I stretched out to enjoy having a little space between me and the probably harmless, total stranger on my row. I began to think about how this seat was all paid for. I thought about how the seat was assigned to James by name and yet, we took off to our destination without him. I also thought about you, dear reader, and how, as you are preparing to fly in life, it's important that you occupy the right seat.

"Great men and women are only born for the time when they are needed the most...."
-Dr. Matthew L. Stevenson, III

Every person born is equipped with answers in the form of spiritual gifts, innate abilities, and a unique personality. These "answers" are sent to empower their generation and to secure the future of the next generation. Simply put, you are a gift and the gifts in you are time and location sensitive. There is power in you that will never be fully activated until you arrive at the right place at the right time. In my family, we call that finding the proper context for your divine content.

Whenever a coaching client is feeling stuck, I lead them in an examination of their physical location. "Are you where your gift is needed? Is there a demand for what you have or who you are in your present surroundings?" The elevation God has for you begins with you being found in the right location. It matters what city you live in. It matters which church you choose to join. It matters what neighborhood you choose to buy a home or apartment.

> *The Lord had said to Abram, "Leave your native country, your relatives, and your father's family, and go to the land that I will show you. 2 I will make you into a great nation. I will bless you and make you famous, and you will be a blessing to others. 3 I will bless those who bless you and curse those who treat you with contempt. All the families on earth will be blessed through you."* Genesis 12:1-3 NLT

This is the first promise God made to the father of our faith, Abraham. It's HUGE and both Christians and Jews are a part of that promise being fulfilled to this very day. Take note of the fact that this promise was predicated by a directive to change locations. I am not telling you to become unstable or to drop everything and be a nomad. But I am saying this...sometimes the blessing is in the blessed place and the promise is in the promised land.

One time I arrived at the airport quite early. My flight was delayed, so I found my gate and some good food, opened my MacBook, popped in my earphones, and started working and eating. Time passed. A lot of time passed. Eventually, I thought, "This plane should be boarding soon and there's been no announcement." Also, I was traveling with two other people and neither of them had arrived. I got that sinking feeling in the bottom of my stomach that something was off.

Right on cue, an announcement began, "Attention passengers. Once again, if you are checked in to flight 1764 to Washington, DC, your gate has changed. If you look around and don't' see anyone you're traveling with it is because you are at the wrong gate! Your new gate is…"

Without moving my head, I glanced up and noticed the people around me were all new faces! At first, I thought it was because I was so early. Then I realized the people who were there when I sat down had all gone to another terminal. Not another gate, another TERMINAL! If I was going to fly that day, I had to get up and move. Alarmed and slightly embarrassed that the gate agent had obviously made a special announcement just for me, I grabbed my things and ran to the correct terminal. I made it and was the last one to board. The moral of the story is this, your place of waiting is not always your place of elevation. Sometimes you are prepared in one "gate" but will fly out of another. So, when the gate agent says move, move!

A Letter to the Exiles

Jeremiah wrote a letter from Jerusalem to the elders, priests, prophets, and all the people who had been exiled to Babylon by King Nebuchadnezzar. 2 This was after King Jehoiachin,[a] the queen mother, the court officials, the other officials of Judah, and all the craftsmen and artisans had been deported from Jerusalem. 3 He sent the letter with Elasah son of Shaphan and Gemariah son of Hilkiah when they went to Babylon as King Zedekiah's ambassadors to Nebuchadnezzar. This is what Jeremiah's letter said: 4 This is what the Lord of Heaven's Armies, the God of Israel, says to all the captives he has exiled to Babylon from Jerusalem: 5 "Build homes, and plan to stay. Plant gardens, and eat the food they produce. 6 Marry and have children. Then find spouses for them so that you may have many grandchildren. Multiply! Do not dwindle away! 7 And work for the peace and prosperity of the city where I sent you into exile. Pray to the Lord for it, for its welfare will determine your welfare." Jeremiah 29:1-7 NLT

I don't know about you, but if I was in captivity in a foreign land and my nation's prophet sent a message, I'd expect to hear something like "You're getting out soon." "Your breakthrough is coming" or "It won't be long now!" That is actually what the false prophets had been telling the Israeli people who were exiled to Babylon. The word they received from Prophet Jeremiah was what I call a future-focused life plan. Build a house? Plant gardens? Get Married? Have Children!!!! Whatha!?! Then, for those who have yet to realize they are going to be in Babylon for more than a few years, this Prophet starts speaking to them generationally. He told them to find spouses for their children! Jeremiah made it very clear that it was the will of God for those Jews to stay in Babylon. And they did stay for over 70 years.

Sometimes, as you are getting ready to fly, God will tell you to stay in a place that you really want to leave. He will give you the same instructions He gave to His people in Jeremiah 29. Stay, build a life, and seek the peace and prosperity of the place where you are. In other words, be an asset, not a liability. Just because you don't want to be in a place, doesn't mean everyone who comes into your presence needs to know and feel it. And since we're being real with each other, let's admit this, the main reason most of us want to leave a place is because "WE" are not there.

We are most comfortable when we are surrounded by people who remind us of us. For the most part, the first thing we do when we walk into a room is look for ourselves. When we consider a new job, school, neighborhood, or city, we want to see someone who reminds us of us. Seeing ourselves makes us comfortable because it gives us someone to relate to. It tells us we'll be safe there. After all, if they can make it here, I can make it here. To this day, I still find myself wishing I had more people like me when I show up in a place. I am often the only woman, the only Black person, the only Christian, the only Pentecostal, the only person over 50, I could go on and on. But, I've learned to get over it.

God sends people to the places they are needed. If YOU are already there, the need would be met. Remember, you are an answer. Even if you are surrounded by people in your exact demographic, (age, race, marital status) they are not you. God told the exiles in Jeremiah 29 to keep their customs and maintain their culture. So, as you are growing stronger and building your life, don't try to blend in with those around you. The authentic you is what is needed. The authentic you is who God will come for. The authentic you is who will fly!

For I know the plans I have for you," says the Lord. "They are plans for good and not for disaster, to give you a future and a hope. Jeremiah 29:11 NLT

"YOU'RE UNDERPAID. It has nothing to do with your gift. It has everything to do with how you see your gift. How you see yourself." These words were spoken to me prophetically in October 2016. One of my specialties is helping people see themselves rightly. My mission statement is "helping people become God's original idea of themselves, thus giving the world better leaders." So, you know I was SHOOK to understand that I was leaving wealth on the table because I didn't see myself rightly. All that year I had been asking God about my increasing my territory. I needed room for my purpose to unfold. I wanted to elevate to a safe space to become more of me. As I stood there hearing those words "It's how you see yourself," I realized I was missing a part of the picture.

It's easy to understand when you need new or bigger territory in order to fly. We've all had that "I need a little room to grow" feeling. However, getting ready to fly is not only dependent on finding the right location but also on embracing the right identity spiritually and emotionally. I had already been using medical research that proved it. I have a breakthrough theory that I use in coaching called, "BE. Do. Have." When a client has something that they want to have or achieve, we reverse engineer that desire and examine who they will need to be in order to win. From there, we work on what Dr. Maxwell Maltz calls the self-image.

Dr. Maxwell Maltz was a successful plastic surgeon, who at the age of 61 published a finding based on over 10 years of study. The study concluded that people are who they imagine themselves to be. Dr. Maxwell Maltz is known for coining the phrase "self-image" and the notion that if your inner self does not equal your outer self, you will always revert back to where you think you belong. The inner self will win every time. Dr. Maltz finally concluded that "self-image" is the key to human personality and human behavior. Change the way we see yourselves and you change the personality and the behavior.

If God brought me out to new territory that turned out to be a large place, but I still saw myself as small, I would never possess my possessions. I would revert back and desire the small, comfortable place because that is how I would see myself. The same is true for you. If you follow the directives of God concerning your physical location, finding the right seat, but you fail to shift internally, you may never have what you're working so hard for because you failed to first become the person to possess it.

> *For as he thinks in his heart, so is he.*
> *Proverbs 23:7 NKJV*

A Biblical example of my "Be. Do. Have" theory is found in the heartbreaking story of the freed Israeli slaves. After enduring more than 400 years of brutal slavery, the nation of Israel did not diminish; they multiplied and preserved their culture. When it was time to leave Egypt, God sent a prophet, Moses, to lead them out. It must have felt like a dream come true! God showed them His power to provide for them and to protect them from their enemies as they headed towards "The Promised Land." (Whether or not you believe the Bible, you really should read this story. The book of Exodus is full of success principles!) The heartbreak came when they arrived at the edge of The Promised Land. It was everything good they had ever heard, hoped, or dreamt. They saw the land exactly right, but they saw themselves exactly wrong. Moses sent twelve courageous men to spy out the land. Two of them returned saying "It's just as God said, let's go in!" The other ten came back saying "It's just as God said, but there are giants there, and compared to them, we are like grasshoppers." Unfortunately, the people believed the ten and broke their hearts from disappointment. After generations of suffering and decades of wandering, their self-image prevented them from receiving the promise. They wept all night feeling that God had dashed their hopes and dreams. But the promise of God was right before them.

This generation who had survived such hell and had endured such suffering could never receive what Heaven had promised them. Because of their unbelief, the entire nation of people was sentenced to wander around a desert until all but two of the original freed generation had died off. That took another forty years.

Eventually, the nation was made up of only those who had been born in the wilderness. They had never felt the whip of the slave master on their backs and had never seen themselves as slaves. They had a different self-image. This generation, plus the two men who had been preserved because of their faith, took possession of The Promised Land only because they were able to see themselves as possessors and not slaves.

What have you lived through hell for? What promise are you expecting? As you are preparing for elevation on the outside, make sure you are allowing your self-image to evolve as well. In fact, your self-image needs to evolve at a faster rate than your change in location or status. This is a must in order to provide the determination and the energy you will need to take possession of your promise. It will also develop the heart you will need to steward it well.

Noblesse Oblige

One of the very best stories on taking the right seat is about a man named Mephibosheth. (He is introduced parenthetically in 2 Samuel 4:4) When King David came into rulership, he wanted to keep his word to his covenant friend, Jonathan. Jonathan's father, Saul, had been king before David. Even though Saul was David's mortal enemy, yeah, he actually tried several times to kill him, David had a brotherhood and a covenant of kindness with Jonathan that extended beyond Jonathan's death.

After David took the throne as king, he asked Ziba, someone, who used to be on Saul's staff, if there was a descendant of Jonathan or Saul to whom He could show kindness. Ziba said, "Yes, it's Mephibosheth, he was dropped, he's crippled." King David sent for him and invited him to his table. Actually, David invited Mephibosheth into a whole new life.

> Don't be afraid!" David said. "I intend to show kindness to you because of my promise to your father, Jonathan. I will give you all the property that once belonged to your grandfather Saul, and you will eat here

with me at the king's table!" 2 Samuel 9:7 NIV

We love this story because we can all relate to the underdog, Mephibosheth. We can relate to being dropped, injured, or even feeling handicapped in life. We can relate to feeling unworthy or uneasy about receiving kindness from a powerful person who owes us nothing at all. It reminds me so much of our relationship with God as Father. Because of the New Covenant Jesus introduced, we now can receive unearned favor from God who is all-powerful. We call it grace and it can be one of the most uncomfortable truths to understand. There is nothing-no rules, dress code, offerings, or acts of service, you could ever do to qualify for the kindness God shows us. It simply has to be received. [For more on grace, I highly recommend reading the book, Church Clothes, by Dr. Matthew Stevenson]

Can you imagine yourself in King David's seat? Getting ready to fly will not only require you to take your seat at tables when you've been invited, but God will also require you to build and prepare your own tables. As God elevates you, He wants to make you a king. Can you imagine yourself as the powerful person who extends the invitation to the broken to eat with you at your table?

"Everyone who has been a Mephibosheth will one day need to be a David."-Pam Ross

Noblesse Oblige is a French phrase, literally translated "Nobility Obligates." In English, we use it to express the responsibility of those with privilege, celebrity, or success to be generous to their community. This is greater than the principle of "paying it forward" because it applies regardless of what others have done or have not done for you. Those of us who believe in Noblesse Oblige never take on a "tit for tat" attitude. "Well, no one ever helped me, so I don't need to help anyone else." "People need to pull themselves up by their own bootstraps!" I have a particular distaste for that one.

Rather than paying "what you owe," Noblesse Oblige teaches that a part of the purpose of your success, wealth, or influence is to solve problems, relieve suffering, and to facilitate righteousness. We see examples of this in modern-day royals who take up a cause. From what I've observed, the Kennedy family is a strong example of this in America. Their family is responsible for establishing the Special Olympics, The Peace Corps, The Kennedy Center, and The Kennedy Foundation. There is an obligation upon those of us who consider ourselves a part of the royal family of God. Jesus taught this concept to his followers. "When someone has been given much, much will be required in return; and when someone has been entrusted with much, even more, will be required." (Luke 12:48)

God wants to make you a benefactor. Remember the original promise to Abraham? "[2] I will make you into a great nation. I will bless you and make you famous, and you will be a blessing to others." If you take the wrong seat, the seat of entitlement, you will be waiting for the blessing to come to you. You won't see yourself as the one who IS the blessing. You'll be waiting for someone else to come along and solve the problems you were sent to solve. I love prayer. I believe in prayer. At the time of this writing, I am responsible for the culture of prayer in over 20 churches. However, there is a time to pray for answers and there is a time to BE the answer. It is vital that you know the difference, or you will miss the purpose of your elevation and fly at a low altitude.

I taught a course in Bible college titled, "Breaking the Spirit of Poverty." In the very first class, the students were challenged to write down what problems they wanted to solve based on the scripture Ecclesiastes 10:19 Money answers all things. All of the students began by clearing their debts. Most moved on to establishing a life of comfort and safety for themselves and their families. A few of them began to list ways they wanted to enrich their world. "Donate to medical research." "Upgrade the schools in my neighborhood." One even wrote, "Improve conditions in senior citizen's homes." After the assignment was complete, I said, "I'm now going to distribute the appropriate amount of wealth, opportunity, and talents to each of you so you can do all that you wrote down." Some of them received little because they desired to do little. Others received a lot because they desired to do so much more. The students understood that true wealth has little to do with what you have and everything to do with what you are willing to do with what you have. If you're going to take the seat of King David, would you build a table for more than one?

Take a look around at your world. Like Mephibosheth, people have been dropped. People are broken.

People are crippled and forgotten. If you are thinking small about yourself, your response to the pain of the world will sound like this. "Isn't that a shame. Dear God, please send somebody to help those broken, forgotten people." But if you receive and understand your noble obligation, your response will sound something like this. "Because I'm royal because I'm privileged because I'm favored, I have an obligation to help someone, even if it's just one person."

> *The whole city celebrates when the godly succeed; they shout for joy when the wicked die. Proverbs 11:10 NLT*

A Gentle Warning

When you decide to take the seat God has for you, you may experience an immediate sense of inferiority. This feeling is often referred to as Impostor Syndrome. Impostor syndrome is a way of thinking that causes one to doubt their accomplishments and leads to a fear of being exposed as a fraud. The truth is, most if not all successful people have experienced this at one point or another. It is important that you learn to recognize and silence impostor syndrome, so you won't abdicate your seat.

Isaiah 55:8-9 says that God's thoughts are HIGHER than ours. From that, we know that God's dreams, ideas, and purposes for each of us are immeasurably higher than we imagine. So, when we take the seat God selects for us, it's natural to feel like it should be for someone else.

There are commonly five types of dysfunctions born from impostor syndrome. Here is a brief description and my advice for each.

1. The Perfectionist: She sets excessively high goals; feels defeated when she misses the mark. My advice: recognize there is no such thing as 100% perfect. Nobody expects you to be Mary Poppins.

2. The Superman/woman: This workaholic is determined to prove their worth even at the risk of relationships and health. My advice: make your life bigger than your work, everyone around you will love you for it.

3. The Natural Genius: Even worse than the perfectionist, this one harshly judges himself for not getting things perfect the first time. My

advice: "Do or do not, there is no try" was great advice from Yoda, but you are not a Jedi warrior. So try new things and learn to enjoy the process of getting better at something new.

4. Soloist: This one feels like asking for help is worse than getting it wrong. She works alone so others won't detect any weaknesses. My advice: Christianity is a team sport, build a team.

5. Expert: His worst nightmare is that someone else may know something he does not. I Cor 8:1 teaches that knowledge makes us feel important. Learn to follow your passions but disconnect the pride.

If you find yourself in any of these categories, use the GRTF Personal Flight Guide, it can help you identify how these dysfunctions are showing up in your life and give you the tools to overcome each of them.

I've said for years, God has a dream of you. He sees you as the person He created in His image and His likeness. God also has a dream for you. There is an abundant life, full to overflowing that has already been prepared for you. You may have to find the location He has for you or stay in the place of development and preparation. But most importantly, don't abdicate your seat. Take your seat of authority, love, solution, or resource. The world needs YOU.

Congratulations! You've checked your bags and you've found your seat. In the next chapter, fasten your seatbelt because sometimes these take-offs can be a little rocky.

Fasten Your Seatbelt

Make a Decision

"Ladies and gentlemen, this is your final opportunity to deplane before the flight crew closes the doors and we head to beautiful Honolulu, Hawaii." My entire face lit up, first with panic-I'm supposed to be headed home from a work trip. Then with sheer delight, I thought, " I could pretend to have been sleeping, and having not heard the announcement, I ended up on the beach. Yeah, my boss would buy that, right?" "Juuust kidding, we'll have you on the ground in Chicago in two and a half hours," the cheery flight attendant said. I didn't think it was very funny, but I fastened my seatbelt and committed to head home to Chicago.

Seatbelts are not designed to protect you in a crash. They are designed to secure you safely in your seat during turbulence. Most flights experience varying amounts of turbulence ranging from light, moderate, severe, or extreme. This is why before every flight you'll see flight attendants walk down the aisle ensuring that each and every passenger has their seatbelt fastened.

In fact, the plane won't even take off until every single person has their seatbelt securely buckled. This communicates to the cabin crew that you are committed to the flight and ready to take off. For our purposes, seatbelts represent your commitment to the process of elevation.

In the previous chapter, we took our seat and said "Yes" to our true identity. Once you agree with God that you are who He says you are, He can accelerate the process of developing you into the fullness of that identity. Your agreement with God is necessary, and your commitment to remain in your identity is paramount because you will experience various types of turbulence. Let's compare these descriptions of turbulence from weather.gov with your rise to success.

Light turbulence momentarily causes slight changes in altitude and/or attitude or a slight bumpiness. Occupants of the airplane may feel a slight strain against their seat belts.	You feel uncomfortable or queasy at the thought of pursuing success. Fear of change, criticism, rejection, or being taken advantage of might arise. Keep breathing and move forward.

Moderate turbulence is similar to light turbulence but somewhat more intense. There is, however, no loss of control of the airplane. Occupants will feel a definite strain against their seat belts and unsecured objects will be dislodged.	Insecurities surface. You may feel out of place as you ascend. People and things may start to drop out of your life. Remain calm and trust the process.
Severe turbulence causes large and abrupt changes in altitude and/or attitude and, usually, large variations in indicated airspeed. The airplane may momentarily be out of control. Occupants of the airplane will be forced violently against their seat belts.	External factors appear to hinder your progress. You may experience failure or a slow season. Self-doubt will arise. Remember who you are! Remember why you're there.
In extreme turbulence, the airplane is tossed violently about and is impossible to control. It may cause structural damage.	Your life feels totally out of control. You want to quit. You may encounter significant life changes, i.e. death, divorce, loss or change of job, or ending or rearranging of alliances. Don't make any sudden

	decisions. Keep your wits about you and listen for instructions.

But Jesus told him, "Anyone who puts a hand to the plow and then looks back is not fit for the Kingdom of God." Luke 9:62 NLT

You will need something to hold on to during the "turbulence" of life. When life seems a little scary or very terrifying, my favorite thing to hold on to is a decision.

The root word for decision is "cis" or "cid." It means "to cut off." From it, we get words like incision, scissor, and circumcision. To be decided is to have the power to cut off options. It is having the mental strength and the intestinal fortitude to cut off what is less important and embrace what is truly essential. I often say the undecided can't stand the sight of blood! Keeping all of your options open is a dangerous thing. It's like flying in an airplane with the door open and your seatbelt unbuckled. You're going to get bounced around.

At the time of this writing, I have been consulting and training for over 20 years. Over the last two decades, I went from "Who is Pam Ross?" to "Hey, you're Pam Ross!" When I first started speaking and training, I would be super excited for every invite. "They want me?!?" I would exclaim. My answer was always yes and off I went. I was taking selfies on every plane and living the dream. Eventually, those requests became numerous. I had very few days off and a little recovery time. On the brink of being overwhelmed, I had to become a decisionmaker.

Decisionmakers are skilled at cutting away excess so that they can be fully committed to the right things. As you elevate you will have increased options and being decisive will be your number one tool to ensure an honest commitment. It is an honor to be sought after, but remember you are not built for every task or every audience. Develop your process for determining if an opportunity is really for you. Base that process on your real identity, not on who people want you to be. This will help you make strong decisions and will stabilize you in elevation. It could even put you on a winning streak.

A relatable example of a commitment process is a man named Gideon. He lived in Israel during a time of tremendous oppression. Three foreign armies invaded his country resulting in poverty and desolation. His people were left with nothing, no herds, no crops, no freedom, and no hope. An angel appeared to Gideon and greeted him as "Mighty Man of Valor." Talk about a new identity! Gideon was the smallest in his family, which was the smallest family in his tribe, which was the smallest tribe in Israel. After a. series of tests, Gideon took a seat in his new identity as a Mighty Man of Valor. That's when the turbulence began.

Gideon recruited 32,000 men to fight against his oppressors and deliver his people. But God told him he needed to cut the team. He had to cut the team to ensure the identity of "Mighty Man of Valor" was preserved. First, he cut everyone who was afraid. 22,000 men voluntarily went home because fear and valor don't mix. Gideon was left with only 10,000 men. Then God spoke again.

> But the Lord said to Gideon, "There are still too many men. Take them down to the water, and I will thin them out for you there. If I say, 'This one shall go with you,' he shall go; but if I say, 'This one shall not go with you,' he shall not go." Judges 7:4 NIV

As you rise, God will make decisions about you. He will cut out or cut off anything that would prevent you from being the person you've agreed to be. Some things you will understand and others you may not. The King James version of Judges 7:4 reads ⁴...the Lord told Gideon. "Bring them down to the water and I'll refine them for you there." (emphasis added) Refine is the Hebrew word Tsarap. The Cornerstone Biblical Commentary offers this clarity.

The verb refers to the smelting and refining of precious metal by heating it and skimming off the slurry of waste material that comes to the surface.

God wasn't reducing Gideon's army simply for the sake of size or to keep them from bragging. He was refining it to its purest form. Throughout the Bible, we find references to God and His word as a refiner's fire (Psalm 12:6, 1Peter 1:7, Psalm 66: 10-12). Refining is what He does to those He intends to elevate and it is never, ever comfortable. Refining causes things we'd rather hide, ignore or deny, to bubble up to the surface. We'll see these things in our personality, words, and actions. The refining process isn't necessary so we can see how terrible we are. No, it is not about disqualifying us. Refinement is necessary so that we can see how merciful God is and allow Him to heal us and make us fit for our destination.

In Luke 9:62, Jesus describes the Undecided as, "not fit for the Kingdom of God." He isn't saying that the Undecided are bad people. Rather that it is the Decided who become fit. The decision makes you fit because the Decided are committed to the process.

We Are Committed

When I was a little girl, around six or seven years old, I had a terrible fear of heights. This phobia didn't interfere with my everyday life. Thankfully, my school, girl scout meetings, and dance classes were all on the ground level. This phobia was discovered, faced, and conquered on the playground swings. The unusual thing about it was that I didn't avoid the swings, in fact, I enjoyed them. I just wanted, or rather needed to be in total control of both the height and the speed of the swing at all times. So, you may have cheery memories of parents, siblings, or friends pushing you on the swing, but I don't.

If someone saw me on my swing, pumping away with my little legs trying to get to juuuust the right height, they would stop and offer to give me a push. "NO!" I'd shout, "Don't push me!" My older sister, Marilyn was employed as my swing guardian. She would make sure no one with good or bad intentions snuck up behind me to offer help. I loved the fun of swinging, but I didn't want to go beyond my personal comfort level.

I was so determined to maintain my comfort that if my swing got too high, I would leap out of it! Just imagine. I would thrust my little body forward, arms and legs flailing wildly through the air. I scraped knees and elbows, risking life and limb. But I didn't worry about injury. I just hated the feeling that happened in the pit of my stomach every time the swing got just a little too high.

Interestingly enough, I still get that same feeling in my stomach when my life is about to level up. I've stood backstage or sat side-stage waiting for my name to be called with my heart pounding so hard I wondered if the lapel microphone would pick up the sound. Every ounce of me wanted to run to the nearest exit. Eventually, I discovered that jumping out is more dangerous than riding it out. I just say to myself, "Girl, you can't get out of this now; you're committed."

> *Commit everything you do to the Lord. Trust him, and he will help you. Psalm 37:5 NLT*

Flying requires a commitment to both speed and height. The average commercial runway is between 8,000 and 13,000 feet. Within this space, the pilot must hit a particular speed known as V_1. It is a decision speed beyond which take-off should not be aborted. Once the plane achieves V_1, the pilot is said to be "committed." The instruments or the copilot will inform him "Captain, you are committed." Even though the plane is still on the ground, it is going too fast to safely stop. It's going to fly.

As you are preparing your life for elevation and success, things that seemed fun, like that playground swing, may start to feel frightening because you're going higher and you're moving faster. Doing cooking demos on your private YouTube channel was fun. But when a publisher calls and asks if you'd write a cookbook, things can get scary. You may even long for the days when things were smaller.

There is a speed in every elevation story when you are working extremely hard on the ground. You grind for every win. You push for every ounce of success and every inch of progress. As hard as this speed is, many people on the other side of it refer to it as "the good old days." Years ago, my children and I lived in a small rental house where I slept on a futon in my home office. I look back on that season and although the work was hard and resources were few, life was simpler. I paid fewer taxes. I had one calendar and one email address, and I was my own administrator. Those were my good old days.

I developed my prayer life in the good old days. I built the culture of my team in the good old days. I solidified my key friendships in the good old days. My leadership muscles were built in the good old days. The Bible teaches us not to despise the day of small beginnings. (Zechariah 4:10) However, it is never the plan of God for us to stay small.

On the other side of the grind of the good old days is the momentum of success. This is when you're no longer carrying your dream, now your dream is carrying you. It can be glorious and a little bit scary. It's natural to feel out of control when momentum kicks in. You know God wants to take you beyond your wildest dreams. However, when you catch a glimpse of the height of that plan, you may struggle to trust Him to keep you safe all the way up there. This is when commitment will become your seatbelt and keep you from bailing out.

Maximizing momentum is about shifting from one form of energy, your own, to divine energy by partnering with God. That means, you are now following His plan for your life, even if it means abandoning your smaller, safer plan. It is the only way to safely soar. it is the only way to be unstoppable. I often say it would be easier to stop a moving train than to stop a believer who partners with the plan of God for her life.

The gift of personal momentum is given to you when you partner with what God wants to do in your life. Prophet Kevin Leal

Yes, building up momentum is hard work and it requires commitment but as you partner with God he will carry you and you will achieve the lift you need to take flight and Soar!

Warning, Seatbelts Restrict Your Movement

"Truly, I tell you[i] emphatically, when you were young, you would fasten your belt and go wherever you liked. But when you get old, you will stretch out your hands, and someone else will fasten your belt and take you where you don't want to go. John 21:18 ISV

The above passage is part of a conversation Jesus had with Peter, a lead member of his team. Jesus was describing how Peter's death would give glory or ascribe honor and power to God. This passage has always meant more to me than natural death. It is a picture of maturity and surrender.

Our relationship with God develops similarly to any other relationship. In the beginning, when things are young and everything is new, we "fasten our belt" because we are going where we want to go. We commit because we believe the relationship will take us to the peace, prosperity, and health we desire. And it works! New faith seems to work quickly. I've seen new believers pray for a speckled puppy and somehow, God arranges for somebody somewhere to show up at their workplace with a speckled puppy who just happens to need a home. God is demonstrating His patient and faithful character to us and responding to our discipline in prayer. However, as we mature, we have to lean less into receiving from God and more into knowing Him. Our motive becomes less about our own pleasure and more about His glory.

Just as Jesus spoke to His friend Peter about how his death will bring God glory, the mature believer experiences a type of death in the elevation process. We die to wanting everything our way. We die to our preferences about who we help or who helps us. We die to our insecurities, pride, and protecting our reputation. Most importantly, we die to our fears.

I can't count the number of times I've flashed my eyes to the sky and said, "This is KILLING me!" all the while knowing I was in the perfect will of God. - @pRthebuilder

Preparing for elevation will cause your schedule and your activities to get a little tight. New interests and passions start to emerge. Your new values will show and those in your social circle will notice. One of my clients let's call him James- decided he would pursue a career as a commercial driver. James lives in a state where marijuana is legal and most of his social activities centered around kicking back and getting high with friends.

James began to gradually feel the internal resistance to smoking marijuana. He knew that the life he wanted, the higher life, (no pun intended), involved random drug tests. Suddenly, something that was legal and enjoyable became unbeneficial to him. Something that he thought he had every right to do, could potentially block his next move. James had to fasten his seatbelt and allow himself to be restricted from doing something that he enjoyed and that others could do without any consequences.

James had to fight for a positive perspective by not comparing his process to that of his friends. If he had allowed seeds of resentment to be planted in his heart, eventually, he would have invented a logical reason to give up his dream. God used James's dream to deliver him for his addiction to marijuana. So, he got off the couch and invested in himself. As a result, he's living a better life now.

This type of restriction will happen to you and you'll be tempted to feel punished by your process. Resist it! When your commitment restricts your activity, you are practicing a level of agency that will be needed in your future. Agency is defined as the capacity of individuals to act independently and to make their own free choices. Don't be a slave to your freedom.

Help is on the way!

Fastening your seatbelt will also activate a very important and indispensable element to your destiny; mentors. No one becomes themselves by themselves, so when you are ready to commit, God will staff your life to ensure safe passage to your next level. And Just like every flight has a different captain, you may have different mentors to take you higher for every elevation. Here are seven ways to spot a mentor and get the most from their appearance.

- Your mentor will influence you: Mentors throw their weight around. They've been there and done that, so they challenge you to go there and do that. Open your mind and be inspired by all the possibilities they present.

- Your mentor will be different from you: Although they are relatable, your mentor will be different from you. Increase your value for diversity. Learn new languages and customs. Seek to understand the culture of where you are going.

- Your mentor will have a sharp knife: Mentors see your future and challenge you to make decisions, (cutaway,) anything that will hinder your healthy elevation. Don't be afraid to look at yourself through their eyes.

- Your mentor will edify you: Edify is a powerful word! It means to build up by instruction. Position yourself as a student when in their presence. Put what you learn to immediate use.

- Your mentor will expand you: With an eye for potential, your mentor will see the endless possibilities of your current gifts. Mentors encourage, by pointing out what you do well and asking for more of it. Be willing to see the extraordinary in what you do naturally.

- Your mentor will transform you: When Jesus met Peter, he said to him, "Follow me and I'll make you a fisher of men." Following the right mentor should make you into your genuine identity. After every encounter, ask yourself what you are applying.

- Your mentor will reveal you: Every mentoring relationship begins with identification and leads to introduction. Mentors reveal who you are, first to you, and then to the world.

Funny Story: The above list is a result of an informal poll of people who have received mentoring, advice, or counsel from me or who are mentors themselves. The most unusual answer I received was Transmute. Yes, I had to look it up! It means to change in form, nature, or substance. Synonyms of transmute are convert, alter, or metamorphose. I'm giving it a special note here because it is the sum of the seven effects listed above. With the right mentor, you will become the next level you, the updated you, the ready you. Being open to allowing the right people in your life to "transmute" you, is a part of elevation. Those who insist on rising alone are fearful, prideful, or idolatrous.

Turbulence is designed to secure your commitment. If you've ever been flying comfortably with your seat belt off and you hear, "Ladies and Gentlemen, the captain has turned on the seat belt sign" that's when you remember to check your decision. Check your commitment even if it restricts your movement for a while. Why? Because the wind outside is about to get rough. When things get rough, that's not when you loosen up a little, that's when you tighten up, a LOT! When things get rough, that's not when you start backing up from your supporting relationships, your community, or your mentors. That's when you come closer, talk more, and listen more.

I've seen people get honest criticism from a loving mentor and pull away from her. They sit in the back of the room. Won't engage in meetings. Give the silent treatment. Correction is meant to help you grow in the right direction and prevent you from growing wild.

Some people go completely ghost, Missing In Action, Absent With Out Leave, call it what you want. When I finally see them again and ask where they've been, this is their answer. "I was really going through some rough things, but I'm better now." What? That is senseless! The people in your life should secure your identity in rough winds. Yes, there are times when you need to be alone. But pulling away from your stabilizing community because you're in a rough season is the equivalent of taking your seatbelt off because your flight is in turbulence. I'll say it again, senseless. Asking for help is not easy for everyone. Neither is admitting fear. Once a friend asked me about my fears and insecurities. I said, "I'm too insecure to talk about my fears and I'm afraid of revealing my insecurities." Funny, yes, but painfully true. If this is you, summon all the courage you can and get the help you need. It helps to realize you're going too fast to stop and you're too high to jump. Here's a passage of me preaching my heart out about being committed to fly.

"I have cut my ties with the lower life and I've got to go higher. I've cut it, I've cut my ties, I'm not going back. I don't have any romantic memories, I don't have any sentimental value of what it was like to be poor and rejected, lost, and depressed. I've cut it and I'm committed. My seat belt is on. I'm at decision speed. I'm too far in now.

I know too much. I know too much about wickedness that I can't go back. There's nothing to go back to. Darkness has nothing for me. If I try to go back, depression, poverty, rejection will kill me and make a trophy out of me. The spirit of darkness would hang my head on a wall and use it as a warning to say, 'See what I do to people that try to advance?'"

Remember little me in the playground swing in the previous chapter? I took on the burden of the process because I wanted to control it. I wanted to use "Pam Power" and stay low rather than allow "pushers" to lift me higher than I could have ever gotten on my own. But that is not you. You are committed to fly. Otherwise, you wouldn't have gotten this far in this book. You're not jumping out of the swing when it gets a little too high. You're not jumping out of the plane when turbulence hits. You are willing and able to ride out your process. Oh! I'm so proud of you already!

Now, can we talk about your appetites?

Tray Tables Up

First Class

In my world there are snacks and then there are "snacky-snacks." Snacks are the things you buy for everyone in the house. They are stored in the pantry in case someone gets hungry between meals, but "snacky-snacks" are those special treats just for me. They may come at a higher price or not be as readily available as most snacks. Snacky-snacks are never, ever found in the pantry. They are secretly stashed in my office or creative space. And because they are so special, very often they accompany me on flights.

On my very first trip to Denver CO, I was invited to facilitate a workshop for the Woman Evolve Conference hosted by none other than Sarah Jakes-Roberts. At that time, this was the most significant opportunity in my speaking career. This trip felt like a reward to me for a lot of reasons. For years I had considered my divorce the greatest failure of my faith. I had struggled to include the narrative in the book, The Force of Joy. Courageously, (well, probably more out of obedience,) I included the testimony in the book. The book served as an introduction for me and the story is what had garnered my first-class flight. So, this occasion called for my favorite snacky-snack, a blend of seasoned nuts with dried fruit and dark chocolate.

After I settled into the luxury of my first-class seat and fastened my seatbelt, I reached for my snacky-snack. "Ms. Ross?" I looked up at the sound of my name. Do flight attendants normally know the names of first-class passengers? "Yes," I answered, locking eyes with the most handsome flight attendant I have ever seen in my life. I mean this guy was... O.K. back to the snack, not him, I mean the actual snacky-snack.

"If you're hungry," he said, "I can bring you something." He returned with a lovely tray holding, among other things, a ramekin of warm nuts that were the best I've eaten. "What would you like to drink?" he asked. "Oh, water is fine," I replied. For some reason, I felt like I didn't want to be a bother. As he turned to get that water, something dawned on me. This was my decision. It is just as easy for him to bring me champagne as it is to bring me water.

"Sir, may I have sparkling water with two limes?" I asked. He smiled as if to say, "Now you're flying first-class."

One of the most wonderful things about elevation is choice. One of the most dangerous things about elevation is also choice. Refining and taming your appetites is a key element in preparing your soul to soar. As your life elevates so should your appetites. It is a wise thing to examine what satisfies you and to understand why. A very effective way to refine and tame appetites is through fasting.

When You FAST

"When you fast, do not look somber as the hypocrites do, for they disfigure their faces to show others they are fasting. Truly I tell you, they have received their reward in full. 17 But when you fast, put oil on your head and wash your face, 18 so that it will not be obvious to others that you are fasting, but only to your Father, who is unseen; and your Father, who sees what is done in secret, will reward you. Matthew 6:16-18 NIV

Fasting is the practice of abstaining from eating food for a period of time. People fast for weight loss, detoxing the body, or simply to give their digestive system a break. Fasting is also a common spiritual practice in most faiths. In the above passage from the Bible, Jesus is delivering The Sermon on the Mount. Think of it as a cultural brief. Jesus was reviewing the norms of the Kingdom of God; what we value, how we treat people, and how we engage in our practices and disciplines. You can read the entire sermon in Matthew 5 and 6.

Jesus said "when" not "if" referring to the practice of fasting. This indicates it was a common practice for the believers of His day. He was bringing clarity on the practice to ensure the purity of the results. In our passage, Jesus had four things to say about fasting.

1. Wash your face
2. Inspect your motives
3. Focus on the unseen
4. Expect a reward

Wash Your Face:
Fasting is not a punishment. The desire or instruction to fast is not an indication that you have done something wrong and need to pay for it. Fasting is a choice. It is choosing to shift your focus, your energy, and your time towards the God who loves you and gives you life! That being the case, there is no need to look as if you're being punished. When you fast, no one should be asking you what is wrong, rather, they should be asking you about your radiant shine.

Those who look to him for help will be radiant with joy; no shadow of shame will darken their faces. Psalm 34:5 NLT

You're fasting from food, not from life. So, wash your face and unless you're at a retreat away from people, you should do your best to present to the world your best self, both physically and emotionally. That means don't have a cranky or hangry (hunger + anger) attitude. Do this so it won't be obvious to anyone, but God, that you're fasting. Fasting is a

private practice. It's an inside job between you, your soul, and God.

Inspect Your Motives:
I thought fasting would make me spiritual; it didn't. Jesus indicated that hypocrites fast too. Another word for hypocrite is pretender or actor. Being a pretender doesn't mean your fast isn't real, it means your motive isn't real. Jesus said that just like actors on a stage, what these pretenders really wanted was the admiration and applause of people. They still do. In our social-media-driven world, people will chronicle their fast with videos and posts so the entire world can see how "spiritual" they are. Thousands of people may be impressed, but God isn't! If you are participating in a fast with your church or group, by all means, encourage each other. But if not, keep it to yourself.

Remember to check your motives daily by asking yourself the following questions.
- If no one asks me about this fast, would I even bring it up?

- How will I gauge the success of this fast?
- How am I feeling about myself during this fast?
- Am I sharing for accountability or applause?

Focus on the Unseen:

When your fasting is spiritual, your focus will be spiritual. As you take the focus off of food, the things we can see tend to lose value, and the intangibles increase in value. The condition of your heart, the quality of your relationships, the strength of your character, and even your mental and emotional health will take precedence. Focusing on the unseen is the pathway to true power and a spirit-led life, two keys to maintaining your sanity in elevation.

True power is the ability to know and govern yourself. It begins with self-discovery. I am an advocate for assessments. Most of them are based on science and are truly helpful. Understanding your personality will help you confront your fears. Understanding your strengths will help you make the greatest contribution. Understanding your weaknesses will allow you to be patient with yourself and build a strong team. Fasting should be a time for inward reflection.

True power is connected with loving and honoring who you are. This requires you to come to grips with how God made YOU. Agreement with what God says about you is real humility. That often happens when you get to the end of yourself. Fasting can accelerate this process. Once you can honor yourself, you can authentically honor others. It makes you a better leader, a better partner, and a better person. One of the greatest compliments I receive is that people feel they can be themselves around me.

For years, I never understood exactly why fasting could help one live a spirit-led life. I knew it was true in my own experience. When I fasted, I could hear the voice of God and sense the leading of God clearly. Fasting brought me answers and helped me resolve issues. I must admit that as a lover of science, not being able to clearly explain the cause of this clarity bothered me, even though I greatly benefited from the effect. A conversation I had with a trusted mentor shed tremendous light on the subject. I never miss an opportunity to teach this revelation I learned from Prophet Kevin Leal.

In the garden of Eden, God gave Adam one restriction and we are all familiar with it. "but of the tree of the knowledge of good and evil you shall not eat, for in the day that you eat of it you shall surely die." Gen 2:17 NKJV. Before breaking this single commandment, Adam and his wife Eve received their knowledge directly from God. They spent time with Him every day. Their decisions and attitudes were no doubt influenced by God's perspective. However, after eating of the tree, and more importantly, receiving the KNOWLEDGE, they were led by their own perspective. The first thing they did was judge themselves wrong for being naked. Adam and Eve were not put out of the garden because they broke God's rules. They were put out because they lost God's influence. They no longer had His perspective; they were now deciding what was good or evil. And we have been deciding ever since.

As your life elevates and your choices expand, you will need a stronger "decider" on the inside of you. Is this the right contract? Is this the right business partner? Should I take this opportunity or wait for the next? There will always be a way that seems right, but do you really want to fly by trial and error? Being spirit-led will give you a higher perspective, God's perspective.

Medicine suggests that when someone loses their sight, their hearing increases. Focusing on the unseen while you fast trains you to walk by faith. The more you hear, the more your faith increases, and the stronger it gets. (Yes, I'm one of those people who believes that God talks to those who follow Him.) This isn't about overriding common sense. It is, rather, about increasing your sensitivity and gaining the advantage of knowing what is not obvious to others.

Expect a Reward:

Carnal people don't fast at all. Pleasing their flesh is their reward. Hypocrites fast to impress people. Applause is their reward. Religious people fast to earn a blessing. Pride is their reward. But Jesus instructed us to fast knowing that God will reward. God is unseen, but His rewards are seen, and they are different for each of us.

- Queen Esther fasted three days for the courage to save her people. (Esther 4:15-17)
- The Prophet Daniel fasted when he felt his prayers were answered. (Daniel 10:1-3)
- Jesus fasted before embarking on His earthly ministry (Matthew 4:1-2).
- I have fasted to increase my faith, for peace, to break bad habits, and for wisdom.

When you fast, don't hesitate to ask God for what you want and need. This keeps your fast from being routine and pointless. This is the very definition of religion. Doing something for religious reasons, means you do it without expectation of real change. But when you have an expectation of reward you will not be disappointed. You will receive clarity, instruction, peace, and focus. You have an expectation not because you are good, but because God is good!

Why You Fast

When your flight is preparing to take off, your tray table is up. In the same manner, when your life is preparing to take off, you may have to go "tray tables up." "Tray tables up" is a phrase that, in my world, translates into "I'm not eating food right now because…. "I am preparing to level up," "I'm getting wisdom from God," "I'm humbling myself," or "I'm getting my body under my control."

Fasting is a way to put your physical body in its rightful place as your servant and not your master. So much about our everyday activity revolves around catering to the needs of our physical bodies. We worry about what we're going to eat and drink or what we are going to wear. Then we compare what we're eating, drinking, and wearing to what everyone else is …well, you get the point. Our society is infatuated with youth and beauty. I could tell you stories of women who have risked their health, jeopardized their lives, and amassed significant debt attempting to reclaim their youth and achieve the perfect body. Only to have that standard of perfection change with the rise of a new celebrity.

It is important to remember that your physical body is a tool to carry out the purposes of your life. I am the first to admit that looking your best will give you confidence and being fit is wise stewardship. Nonetheless, your spirit is the most essential part of you. When functioning properly, your spirit has influence over your soul. The soul houses your thoughts, ideas, feelings, and desires. Consequently, your soul commands your body. This is a healthy chain of command or chain of influence. When things run in reverse, your body is in control. If you've ever had a hangover, you don't need me to tell you the dangers of allowing your body to call all of the shots. No pun intended. The body makes a great servant but a terrible boss, so don't allow it to boss your life.

> We are confident, I say, and willing rather to
> be absent from the body, and to be present
> with the Lord 2 Corinthians 5:8 KJV

When the Apostle Paul wrote that he would rather be absent from the body and be in the presence of God, he was referring to natural death. However, I find a deeper meaning here when applied to fasting. When our attention is absent from the body, it is present with the Lord. When our focus is absent from the body, it is present with the Lord. Most importantly, when our hearing is absent from the body, it is present with the Lord. Fasting enables us to become more aware of the presence of God. It is in His presence where we find joy, comfort, answers, and power.

Fasting decreases the conscious and unconscious listening to the cries of the body and focuses us on what God is saying. When my children were brand new babies. I was always listening for them. No matter what I was doing, every now and then, I'd lift my chin and tilt my ear in the direction of that baby. As they matured, that practice faded. I learned that every cry and whimper didn't require my immediate attention.

When I am fasting, I care for my body, but I am not responding to its every whim. I am listening for the voice of the Lord. The more hunger I feel, the more desperate I become to connect with God.

> *Father, as I move this body from the place of priority, I ask that you cause me to be more present with you. Make me more aware of you as I tell this body what it cannot do. I will not be led by the God of the belly. Lord come on and help me. I need your presence more than my*

food!"-Pam Ross "Get Ready to Fly" 2017

We cannot have priorities. It's impossible. The word itself is a mutation. The actual word "priority" is singular, indicating one thing. Fasting helps you come back to one most important thing. It brings your life into order so you can build with confidence. If you're faced with a tough decision or trying to make an important choice, fast a couple of days. It will help you remember who you are and what's important to you.

At the time of this writing, I live in a "food mecca." I could walk to four grocery stores and over a dozen restaurants. My favorite doughnut shop is just one mile away. Several times a day I'm telling myself, "No, you are not going to have that." It even seems to me that people are especially generous with food when I'm fasting. Even stingy people will offer their food and treats when I'm fasting! It's a perfect opportunity to practice discipline.

Discipline is adhering to a preset decision. If you decide on Monday that you're going to fast until Wednesday, I can promise you that you'll be tempted with food on Tuesday. Now a shaky, unstable person will try to make the same decision all over again.

"Now, let me see, do I want this food, or do I want to continue with my fast?" Hilariously, both statements are true. I want this AND I want to continue this fast.

Conversely, a disciplined person will simply adhere or stick to what he has already decided. "I'm going to eat on Wednesday at 6 p.m. so the answer is already NO." Now, how brilliant is that?! You make the decision one time and the rest is just sticking to it. This level of discipline trains the body to wait and wait patiently. Patience is an important key to the elevated life.

I've interviewed a lot of people and will tell you this. Every successful artist, entrepreneur, leader, and partner in a relationship has told me that patience is key to elevation. Something can already be yours and you know it's coming to you. But if you reach for it too soon it could lead to disaster. If you give up because it seems to be taking too long, you would forfeit a guaranteed win. Fasting trains you in perseverance.

Nothing Tastes as Good as a Breakthrough!

One time I was fasting and believing God for a major change in my life. Somebody asked me if I wanted something to eat. I said, "Yes I do. But, you know, nothing tastes as good as a breakthrough." Have you ever said something so good, you knew it didn't come from you? That answer was wisdom for me out of my own mouth. I have never let that mantra go. And I have found it to be true, nothing tastes as good as a breakthrough.

When my stomach growls, I say "Nothing tastes as good as a breakthrough." When my headaches, I say, "Nothing tastes as good as a breakthrough." I will not forfeit the benefit of priority, discipline, and patience for a bowl of beans or a bacon sandwich! My future, my legacy, my life is worth more than that.

Breakthrough happens when the truth we have on the inside of us begins to change how we think. New thoughts create pressure against what you're doing that eventually push us to change our behavior. This change in behavior alters our lives. Voila! You've achieved a breakthrough. Think differently, act differently, have different.

A Breakthrough is a term we use when you move past the barrier of what you know and allow it to affect what you do and say. Have you ever felt the tension of knowing something was true but being unable to access it or live it? You know you should spend less and save more. You know you should watch less TV. You know you should forgive and move on. If you feel there is a chasm between what you know to do and what you are actually doing. You are not crazy. You are not weak. You are not alone. You need a breakthrough.

> *I do not understand what I do. For what I want to do I do not do, but what I hate I do. Romans 7:15 NIV*

Fasting is not easy or enjoyable. I've heard people talk about how fasting gets easy for them after day three. Not me! On day three, I am as hungry as a hostage! So why do I do it? Why have I made this a practice in my life? Why is it one of my secret weapons for elevation? Because no matter how focused you are or how secure you are in your identity, no matter how disciplined or committed you are, some things only change by prayer and fasting.

Just like the Apostle Paul described in Romans chapter 7, verse 15, we all find ourselves doing things we hate. I'm right there with you, overeating, wallowing in rejection, acting out of insecurity, or falling into depression. My list goes on and on. Paul found himself at war with himself. Fasting is not a method to show myself who's boss and bend my lower will to my higher will. NO! Fasting humbles me and brings me to the end of my will. My breakthrough in fasting comes from looking away from me, recognizing that my answers are not in me. Fasting causes me to look to God. He is the Breaker. He brings the breakthrough.

Someone once asked me if my discipline had ever failed me in fasting. Of course, the answer was yes! Once I was on a fast and wanted to put a whole double cheeseburger in a blender! When my children were very young, I wouldn't serve them meat while I was fasting because I love meat so much. Instead, I would put a little scripture card on their plate, right next to their green beans and potatoes where the meat would normally be. I would tell them "Girls, you get to fast with Mama and have the meat of God's Word." For them, it was a team sport. For me, it was an admission that meat was my weakness.

Your discipline may fail you, but your desperation won't. If you fail on a fast, do not condemn yourself and for God's sake do not start over. Just get back on schedule. And remember that NOTHING TASTES AS GOOD AS A BREAKTHROUGH.

Silence Your Communication Devices

Airplane Mode

"The passenger was extremely rude to the crew, calling them inappropriate names and using offensive language."

The verbal exchange between the passenger and the crew on American Airlines flight from Los Angeles to New York got heated. So heated, that despite the seatbelt light being on for departure, the passenger left his seat and hid in the lavatory! He basically grounded the flight. The angry passenger slammed the restroom door so hard and loud; it got the attention of the cockpit crew. That's when the captain got involved. The captain turned the plane around, went back to the gate, and gave orders to immediately escort this unruly passenger off the plane.

What would cause an airline passenger to behave this way? You guessed it. He didn't want to put away his cell phone. Interested parties took to social media and announced to the world that it was American actor, Alec Baldwin, who had been escorted off of the flight. A global debate followed.

The airline released a statement on Facebook and Twitter. The Actor tweeted to his over half a million followers. He later wrote a column in the Huffington Post. Even CNN joined the party and did a 50-sec spot on the news. It seemed everyone had an opinion. Did the flight crew overreact? Was the privileged celebrity out of order? Were the other passengers on their phones? Did the pilot really have to turn the plane around? How did things escalate to this point?

When CNN anchor Brooke Baldwin -- no relation -- tagged Alec Baldwin in a tweet asking about "Words with Friends," the actor replied, "It's, well, addicting."

"Words With Friends" is a multiplayer crossword game similar to Scrabble. I play it just about every day. However, when the doors to the jet bridge close and you're in your seat with your seatbelt on and your tray table up, you just have to silence your communication devices.

We put our phones in airplane mode to ensure the navigation system on our device doesn't interfere with the navigation system on the plane. "Airplane mode" is our metaphor for the conversational changes that happen during seasons of elevation. In the same way that your device can cause static in navigating a plane, listening to the wrong people can waste your time and cause you to lose your way. Promotion requires a change in communication. You must listen differently, talk differently and you must learn to embrace times of silence.

Listen

The year was 1978. My family was traveling from Chicago, IL to Arkansas to visit relatives. We stopped in St. Louis, Missouri in hopes of seeing my uncle W.C. (Yes, that was his actual name.) Mind you, this is before the days when navigation or global positioning systems were installed in every car. It was even before the days of cell phones and we were lost.

My uncle Milton, being a reasonable man, stopped to ask a random guy on the street for directions. Their conversation went something like this.

Uncle Milton: "Hey man! Do you know how to get to 123 ABC Street?

Random Guy: "I don't really know. But if you take this next left and follow the curve, then take a right, you should find it from there."

Uncle Milton: "O.K. Thanks!"

My uncle rolled up the window, then used his rearview mirror to look at us kids in the back seat. "Did you kids get that?" he said. "Nope." I said, "I stopped listening after I heard that guy say, 'I really don't know.'" Even at twelve years old, I knew when to stop listening. Granted, it took me a little longer to learn when to stop talking.

As your life begins to elevate, you cannot take instructions from people who have never left the ground. People who are admittedly on the ground may love you, they may inspire and even encourage you, but they are not equipped to instruct you. Therefore, you will need to learn when and where to lend your ear and when to smile, nod, and keep it moving, respectfully.

The larger your life grows the more people will have an opinion about it. Although they may love you (see my definition of love) their opinions will not always be founded on truth or knowledge. Some opinions will be based on who you were when you were on the ground before you checked your luggage and decided what was most important to you. Their opinions could be generated from their personal fears or cultural norms.

One of my closest friends and advisors was an ultrasound tech at a large hospital. She was highly skilled and well paid with great benefits. Although she had been a teenage mother, she beat the odds and built a successful stable life. Soon, she began to dream about owning her own ultrasound business. She bought equipment and began to work for herself on her days off from the hospital. Ultimately, the time came for her dream to leave the ground. She was going to resign from her job and work for herself. Her father, who loved her dearly, instructed her not to do it.

"It doesn't make sense to leave a good job." her father told her, "You have benefits." As much as my friend loved and respected her father, she chose not to follow those instructions. She took a leap and launched her business, and she has been soaring ever since. Not only did she build a successful business being an expert in her field, today, but she also speaks at conferences and leads a mentoring group for women in business and ministry. She is a role model for women everywhere. Her father was proud of her as well. Even he was happy that she did not follow his "ground-level" advice when she was getting ready to fly. She was a blessing to him until the day he passed away.

Love: contending for the highest good of another

As you are preparing to soar, get direction from people who are in the air above you. Listen for the wisdom of those who have been where you are looking to go. My coach, Anna McCoy, taught me to always look for someone who has done it before and learn their lessons. I have searched out and found both historic and contemporary counterparts. I learn from their feet and build from their shoulders.

Many, many years ago I was returning a phone call to someone at work. I noticed the phone number displayed was one number off from what I meant to dial. I started to hang up, but I heard the voice of the Lord in my heart say "Don't hang up. You need to pray for her." Sure enough, I held on and a woman's voice came on. Thankfully, it was a recording and I could try to leave a message.

"Uuuum, hello. My name is Pam and honestly, I dialed a wrong number, but I heard God say I need to pray for you. So, if you want to, please return my call at......."

The woman called me back and I prayed for her. The prayer was exactly what she needed to hear. Afterward, she told me that she was a minister and invited me to hear her preach at an upcoming event. She sent me the details and I showed up. As I saw her minister, I was drawn in with an unusual laser focus.

After she preached a powerful message, she began to pray for people at the altar. One by one, she laid her hands on the people and they responded powerfully. Suddenly, she stopped and looked directly at me and said, "Prophetess! Come here!" I was completely convinced that she was calling for someone on her ministry team and I knew that person couldn't possibly be me.

Again, she pointed at me and said strongly, "Come here!" This time I looked about, curious to see who she was calling for and why were they so slow in their response. The third time, the impossible happened. "You with the short hair. Come here!" This time it became very clear that she was indeed speaking to me. I went to the altar expecting her to pray for me. What happened next changed my life forever.

She looked at me and said, "You have to be ready!" She then took my hand and began to place it on the next person at the altar. They fell out under the power of God! Together we ministered to every person at the altar.

After service, I remembered that we had not actually met. She still had no idea that I was the woman who called her on the phone. When I introduced myself, she was amazed at what had transpired that night and then said, "You don't know who you are. This is the real you, but you will have to grow into this." Listening to that advice set my course of development to get to my destiny.

To this day, Reverend Constance Jones has been a resource for me. As a woman in ministry and leadership, her advice and instruction have helped me navigate through some of the most confusing and unsettling times in my life.

Honor all. Listen to few. -Pam Ross

The Art of Conversation

Thoughts and ideas are the highest currency on the planet! Your life will lift off based on the elevation of your thoughts and the direction of your ideas. The amount of wealth your life demands will hinge on the quality of your thoughts and ideas. How do you sharpen and elevate your thoughts and ideas? I'm so glad you asked. Higher thinking is the reward of the right conversations.

One of the first things to change as you elevate in life will be the type of conversations you have. Just as you can often tell where someone is from by their accent, you can often tell the level of someone's life by their conversations. I'm not referring to using big words to impress and often confuse the listener. I'm referring to the adage accredited to Eleanor Roosevelt.

"Great minds talk about ideas. Average minds talk about events. Small minds talk about people."

As your conversations elevate, you will spend less time gossiping and speculating about other people. You will scroll (on social media) far less and comment even less than that. You will discover that following your purpose is the cure to FOMO, (Fear of Missing Out). Your interest in what people do will decrease and your interest in why they do it will increase. You will learn to spot trends, connect the dots, and identify cause and effect. That's elevated thinking.

Wisdom Through Conversations

The purpose of conversation is to gain understanding. When approached correctly, conversations can be a well of wisdom for you. Proverbs 4:7 teaches us that wisdom is of utmost importance and in all of our getting to get understanding. Conversations are a perfect tool to fulfill this directive. Right conversations will sharpen, enlighten, challenge, and even correct you. This only happens when you approach a conversation with the motive to learn, to understand, and to be understood. Remember, agreement is not always the target.

You learn to speak the language of where you're going by talking to people who already speak it. Relationships are built through conversation. When you are invited into these key conversations, or as I like to put it "visiting where you really want to live," be ready to build relationships by doing the following.

1. Don't try to be noticed. Instead, focus on noticing others. The smartest people I know are also the most observant. Look around and take note. What cultural cues and patterns can you pick up?

2. Ask good questions. Take advantage of being new by asking open-ended questions. "What do you think about..." fill in the blank with current events, restaurants, or movies.

3. Listen more, speak less. Studies prove we learn more when we shut up. O.K., I'm just kidding. But it is almost impossible to listen and speak at the same time. I love meeting new people because they haven't heard any of my amazing life stories. If you're anything like me, you will need to be intentional about allowing others to get a word in.

4. Be a resource. Look for ways to help others get what they want by connecting them with someone or something you know. It makes you memorable and your connection valuable. Not to mention what goes around comes around.

5. Be kind to everyone. Sometimes the most powerful people are the least assuming. Never, ever be rude to anyone. Be kind to those serving you, like waiters or flight attendants. Remember the names of gatekeepers, like secretaries or executive assistants. Let me give you this wisdom from my grandmother. "If you're kind to everyone, you won't miss the important people."

A Word About Audiences

As you are elevating your language changes. The people that speak your native language won't always understand you, nor will they relate to you. In fact, they may even mock you and feel it's their responsibility to remind you where you came from. This is their fear of speaking. It's easier to believe that life on the ground is just fine than it is to take a risk and endure the process of an elevated life.

Also, your elevation may cause those closest to you to fear losing you. Whenever I take on a coaching client, I ask them to prepare for a shifting in their relationships. We generally attract and become friends with people similar to us. So, when you commit to growth, you will without a doubt, destabilize your existing relationships. Friends and colleagues will react to your growth and elevation in different ways. Some may stay and some may go. Do not abandon your love for these people. Your success just may give them the inspiration they need to prepare their souls to soar.

On the other hand, you may have people who say they are with you, but along the way decide the price is too much to pay or the direction is not what they envisioned. Let them go! Not everyone who started with you is meant to go with you. Remember communication is directly connected to navigation. If you insist on bringing those who are not in agreement with your direction, they may interfere with your ability to navigate.

Elevation can cause loneliness. Feeling misunderstood or isolated can cause extreme emotional pain. Trust me, I've been there. Stay in your seat. That is to say, do not relinquish your identity in God for the acceptance of people. Your difference can be scary to other people. Do not become like them so that they will like you. Instead, embrace your difference. Become the fullness of who you are meant to be. This advice reminds me of King David, one of the greatest heroes in the Bible. He was just a different guy. Everywhere he turned he encountered advice from people who wanted him to just be like them. When their nation's prophet came to his home to anoint the new king of Israel, David's father didn't even call him in from the sheep pasture. He must have thought, "David is too different to be the next king." He was wrong! David was anointed king. When he decided he would face the giant, Goliath in battle, the current king, Saul, offered David his armor. David was willing to try it on, but it just wasn't the right fit for him. He defeated the giant with a slingshot instead. Now, that was different!

Many, many years later, as King David was bringing the Ark of the Covenant back to Jerusalem, he led a parade of praise and danced until his clothes came off. Most kings would have had a parade in their honor. They would have stood in a window and waved at the people as they paraded by. David led a parade in God's honor. His difference drew the criticism of his wife, Michal. She told him that his undignified difference embarrassed her. He didn't say "Oh, honey, I'm so sorry, I should act more like your father, the previous king." NO. He said, "I will become more undignified than this." (2 Samuel 6:22) David leaned into his difference even if it meant ignoring the advice or the criticism of others around him. He is known as a man after God's heart. This means he wasn't pridefully obstinate against people, instead he was humbly focused on God. This is the posture you will take as you silence your communication device. You can't take advice that pushes you into being someone you're not.

Stay committed to the process of becoming more of you than ever before. Eventually, God will send you people to travel with you. And you will identify them because they will speak the language of your destiny.

Silence is Golden

Admittedly, I don't enjoy everything about flying. But one thing I really do enjoy is the necessity to be without my phone. I am one of those folks whose phone is always on, so putting my phone away was like a little mental vacation for me. I started to view time on a flight with my phone on airplane mode as a gift of blank space. I treasured that unclaimed mental space to think, to not think, to just be. I even keep my earphones in my ears, so others won't speak to me.

After a while, I began to create that blank space on purpose whenever I felt I needed it. Putting my phone away is a focus move for me. Here are just a few examples of when I routinely put my phone away and go off the grid.

- Eating a meal. Yes, even when I'm eating alone, my phone is put away. Do yourself a favor and enjoy your meals in gratitude and joy. You'll be healthier for it.

- Entering my home. My drive home can be considered extended office hours because I often work on my commute. When my children were younger, I wanted to come home and be fully present when I arrived home from work. To this end, I developed a habit of finishing calls in my driveway. To this day, even if there is no one home, I will still hang up from any call and enter my home in peace.

- The first hour of every day. I do not touch my phone for one hour after I wake up. It gives me space to address the day on my terms. Take time to set priority for your day before the phone asks for a response or a reaction. When I do this, I feel like the owner of my day.

- The last hour of every day. Two hours before bed is the time to check what is on the next day's calendar, send final communications, plan whatever needs to be planned and then wind down. The final hour is about gratitude and peace. Any late-night texts or emails will be there in the morning.

Awkward

There is no such thing as an awkward silence. We often feel awkward in moments of silence due to the pressure to always be "on." But if you put your ego on mute and focus on understanding the other person, the silence between statements becomes a natural occurrence in communication. There is nothing difficult or uncomfortable about it. Use a moment of silence to process what was just said and then give the other person time to understand your point. That's a real, honest conversation.

I am a self-confessed chatterbox. Being quiet is a discipline I've had to develop. But it's been worth it. When people would ask me how I was doing, I noticed I would answer by telling them what I was doing. After a very deep conversation with a loving pastor, I decided to dedicate time each day to practice silence. During that time, I look for clarity in my soul. I listen to my heart and really know how I am doing where it matters most, deep inside. I ask a series of questions. Do I have any worries? Are there any frustrations? Is there anything I need to resolve? These questions help me to achieve not just quiet but peace and quiet. There is a difference.

Silence is something that everyone, especially leaders, should practice. Practicing silence builds discipline. It takes discipline to sort your thoughts before you say them. It tames the ego, allowing others to share what's going on with them while you listen. Leaders can discover the brilliance in their team by just being quiet. Most powerfully, practicing silence helps to control your tongue.

> *If anyone can control his tongue, it proves that he has perfect control over himself in every other way. James 3:2 NIV*

We all say things we shouldn't, and no one gets it right every time. However, controlling our tongue is the ultimate discipline for elevation. Practicing silence is training for reigning.

If you can be silent, you can resist releasing information too soon. You can also resist releasing information to the wrong people. Everyone doesn't need to know what your next big thing is going to be. When I decided to produce The Culturalist Podcast, my team wanted to release a "coming soon" graphic. I said NO Way, instead we went to work, produced six episodes, and then invited people to go listen. Releasing information too soon puts pressure on you to rush. When you rush, you're more likely to make mistakes. When you're in the company of people who are doing great things, your ego will put pressure on you to say something important to prove your worthiness. Remember this. If you are in the room or at the table, you have nothing to prove and everything to give. Make that your goal to only say that which will contribute or clarify.

Practicing silence builds mental toughness by giving you space to examine and control your thoughts. One of my favorite leadership hacks is to schedule a time to think ordered and creative thoughts. This helps me distinguish the difference between my inner voice from that of God or of the madness around me! I'll say it again communication is about navigation. It matters which voice you listen to.

Practicing silence will strengthen you against competitive jealousy. You don't need everybody to validate you. Constantly looking for validation will keep you from elevation. Get over FOMO (fear of missing out) and mind your business. Remember, you're getting ready to fly. Imagine getting to the airport and being distracted by where everyone else is flying. You'd miss your flight. You don't have time for that.

Our final point on practicing silence is that it will tune your ear to the voice of God. Learning to be quiet in God's presence will give you a tremendous advantage in life. We often get in His presence and just talk and talk and talk and never give him an opportunity to speak to us. Yes. Pour out your heart to God in prayer. He cares about every detail of our lives. But also spend some time in silence because he will speak, and He is the ultimate navigator.

In Case of a Loss of Cabin Pressure…

Catch Your Breath

"In the unlikely event of a loss of cabin pressure, panels above your seat will open revealing oxygen masks. Reach up and pull a mask towards you. Place it over your nose and mouth, and secure with the elastic band that can be adjusted to ensure a snug fit. The plastic bag will not fully inflate, although oxygen is flowing. Secure your own mask first before helping others."

I started writing this book to help you, my beloved reader, recognize the inner work required for sustained success. What you're reading now, the final pre-flight instruction, started off as a footnote. I planned to simply mention, "Oh yeah, in case something unexpected and unlikely happens, just breathe"

However, by the time I sat to write this chapter, everyone, and I do mean EVERYONE on the planet, has come face to face with the "unexpected and unlikely."

Corona Virus 2019, or COVID19, began in Wuhan, China, in December 2019 and quickly became a global pandemic. According to the New York Times, COVID 19 has sickened more than 13.3 million people and at least 578,100 of them have died. This disease attacks its host by arresting the respiratory system and makes it difficult to breathe.

Suddenly, something we have done all of our lives, something we do literally without thinking, something we do in our sleep has captivated our global focus. We have adopted new behaviors and a new language. We have even passed laws all around this one activity. Our entire world just wants to keep breathing.

I wish I could tell you that if you follow my advice and prepare your soul to soar, all will be well on your journey. However, life has a way of delivering its most devastating blows just as you are about to take flight. Regardless of how smoothly your elevation may be going internally, sometimes external factors come into play and serve you a painful blow. Therefore, this book would not be complete, and I would not be a good coach if I did not address the unpredictability of the world around us. Believe it or not, things happen that knock the wind out of you.

How it happens…

If you ever had the wind knocked out of you physically, it probably happened in one of three ways.

- A fall: You landed hard enough on your back to cause temporary paralysis of the diaphragm and you couldn't take the next breath.

- A gut punch: Something hit you hard enough to cause a diaphragm spasm and you lost your breath.

- Respiratory stress: You exerted yourself long and hard enough to run out of breath.

Let's take a look at the parallels between these physical occurrences and the things life can throw at us.

I've Fallen and I Can't Get Up

In the spring of 2020, the county where I lived experienced sudden rainstorms that broke an 8-year record. The home I bought 6 years ago started taking in water. Thankfully, two of my three daughters were home. They along with my mother and I worked for hours vacuuming and dumping water. The rain subsided. The basement dried out and we put some sealant down.

The next day even more rain came. Water was quickly seeping into my home from 8 different areas! I was overwhelmed. Because we were in the midst of the Coronavirus pandemic, my team couldn't come into my house to help me. Thankfully, they brought me additional supplies, wet vacs, fans, dehumidifiers, and food. They even picked up wet things and took them to be washed, dried, and folded.

Once again, my family went to work vacuuming, pumping, and hauling out water in five-gallon buckets. On one of those trips up the stairs, I spilled a little bit of water. I made a mental note to mop it up when I returned, which I quickly forgot. On my way back down the stairs, I slipped. Both of my feet went out from under me and I landed hard on my back. This was the first time I ever had the wind knocked out of me.

In that moment, I didn't think about the uncontrolled water that was still coming into my house. I didn't think about how tired I was or wonder when I could gain control over the situation. My mom was close by and she was saying something to me. I swear, I did not hear or understand her. For those few seconds, the only thing I wanted was my next breath.

In the same way, hitting those steps knocked the wind out of me, you might suffer a fall or a failure that knocks the wind out of you. It's important to give yourself time to catch your breath. Whether you fell because of your mistake or fell into a trap laid by someone else, your priority is to find peace. You need to get your bearings.

The Fall of Man

When we look at the original fall with Adam and Eve, we discover that God asked "Adam, where are you?" Adam did not give God a GPS report of his physical location. He said, "I heard you in the garden, and I was afraid because I was naked; so, I hid." (Gen

3:10) That's a lot of information and none of it says where he was. Let's take a minute and unpack this.

- Adam felt afraid: Emotions are the governors of our decisions. (If you don't believe me, read The Force of Joy, Building an Unstoppable You, also by Pam Ross) When catching your breath from
- a fall identify what you were feeling at or around the time you did whatever you did. This understanding is going to be a powerful tool to break a cycle of unhealthy behavior.

- Adam judged his nakedness: Isn't it interesting that Adam immediately condemned himself for being naked? God said nothing to him about his nakedness and there is no record that the devil did either. Be careful with "I AM" statements when catching your breath from a fall. You are not what you did!

- Adam hid from God: Now we know we cannot escape the presence of God. (Psalm 139:8) Adam had a daily appointment to talk with God and he canceled himself from God's calendar. When you're catching your breath from a fall, understand that you cannot fix yourself in private and then return to God's presence as if nothing happened. You're going to have to address it, not for condemnation or punishment, but for the healing of your soul and restoration of your relationship with God.

The sensation of being unable to breathe can lead to anxiety and there may be residual pain from the original blow. It took time for my body to recover from that fall on the steps. My back was bruised and in significant pain. For three days, all I could do was lay on ice like a fresh trout! I spent most of that time fighting regret. I kept thinking about how I was the one who had spilled the water! Why did I fill the bucket so high? Why didn't I get that spill up immediately?

Not long after the floods, I was looking out my kitchen window and heard the sound of thunder. My head started pounding, my heart raced, and my stomach turned over. "I'm in a full-on fight or flight sequence." I thought to myself. As I watched the light rainfall, I could feel stress rushing through me, creating havoc in my immune system and my metabolism.

As the days progressed, I didn't want to check the weather. The very thought of rain still gave me a headache. I decided to get help. I scheduled time with a therapist and together we began to do some real work. I had to get past blame and condemnation, forgive myself, and get to the business of healing. The first thing I learned was to take a min and examine my injuries. My body had healed, but my soul had not.

The floods came just after I had cleaned and organized my library, creative space, and conference room. I was happy with the work I had accomplished. This place represented my peace and my security in the midst of the global pandemic. It had been invaded by something I didn't see coming and could not control.

Through conversation with my therapist, I discovered a cycle of creating false securities. I am still dismantling those tendencies and coming to grips with the truth that the name of the Lord is my strong tower. There is no need for me to build my own. (Psalm 18:10). I have installed an internal gage that alerts me if my peace and safety are in the wrong place. When I lay down at night, I say to myself "Pam, you are going to sleep peacefully because Jesus is with you. Not because you have money, a man, influence, or a team of people to help you. Your peace and safety are just Jesus."

That physical fall uncovered a fallen area in my soul. You will make mistakes and even perhaps sin during your elevation process. Your innate reaction will be jumping back up and keep moving forward. Don't. Take time to catch your breath. Ask and answer the right questions. Reset your gages and continue to fly!

The Gut Punch

A "gut punch" is an American phrase used to describe an emotion so painful you can physically feel it in the pit of your stomach. It is generally caused by sudden, disappointing news. It could be the loss of a job, a divorce, or the death of a loved one. While a fall represents the things we fall into, a gut-punch represents the things in life that hit us hard enough to take your breath away. An emotional gut-punch will knock the wind right out of you.

> *Then one of the synagogue leaders, named Jairus, came, and when he saw Jesus, he fell at his feet. 23He pleaded earnestly with him, "My little daughter is dying. Please come and put your hands on her so that she will be healed and live." 24 So Jesus went with him.*
> *Mark 5:22-24 NIV*

Jairus was a leader in the synagogue. However, he wasn't coming to Jesus as a religious leader. He was coming as a father. He had faith that Jesus could heal his twelve-year-old daughter who was sick at home. I imagine that he was hopeful. I imagine that he was relieved when Jesus agreed to go to his house. Then he hit some delays.

Between verse 24 and verse 35 a woman who had been sick for twelve years, pressed through the crowd, reached out, and touched Jesus. She miraculously received healing. This would not have been a problem if Jesus hadn't stopped to conduct a full investigation about exactly who touched him. This led to the woman recounting her twelve-year testimony about being so sick and seeing a multitude of doctors. Just as she was about to tell Jesus about all the various treatments and how none of them worked, Jarius's gut-punch was about to arrive.

> While Jesus was still speaking, some people came from the house of Jairus, the synagogue leader. "Your daughter is dead," they said. "Why bother the teacher anymore?" Mark 5:35 NIV

"YOUR DAUGHTER IS DEAD" was the gut punch. I'm sure it took the wind out of Jairus. But what followed next was the most dangerous statement of all. "Don't bother the teacher anymore." It was a statement of hopelessness. Your initial response to losing your breath from a gut-punch could be to lose hope as well. Beware of this! Pain has a voice and that voice has a message. Pain from disappointment will tell you "Don't bother believing." "Don't bother hoping." Some pain will tell you "Don't bother living."

> *Overhearing what they said, Jesus told him, "Don't be afraid; just believe." Mark 5:36 NIV*

Science has proven that when we are invaded with fear, the part of our brain that makes decisions, our executive brain, is drained. Our thinking gets cloudy and we find it hard to focus. Logic is short-circuited, and our memory is dimmed. This was the state of Jairus in that moment, attempting to process this news. Thankfully, he was able to hear the instructions from God, "Only believe."

> *He did not let anyone follow him except Peter, James, and John the brother of James. 38 When they came to the home of the synagogue leader, Jesus saw a commotion, with people crying and wailing loudly. Mark 5:37-38 NIV*

Throw a Pity party!!

I have changed my mind about pity parties! I used to believe that sitting around feeling sorry for yourself was a pathetic waste of time. However, I've learned that it is a good thing to take a moment (not a lifetime) to sit and realize what you've been through. It is a good way to process your pain and examine where you hurt and why. As a leadership coach, I've discovered that many of the dysfunctions we see in leaders are due to unprocessed pain. Entire organizations suffer because of what a leader refuses to face.

When something knocks the wind out of you, don't you dare let some plastic person with a concrete heart tell you to "shake it off." I don't care how tough you think you are. Listen to those who will say "Hey, that was rough. Are you O.K.?" Even better, you need people who will say "Hey, you are NOT O.K."

Professional boxers are trained to take a gut punch and even they get a standing eight count. Also, known as a protection count, a standing eight count happens when a referee stops the fight and gives a boxer an eight-second relief. This can happen even if the boxer hasn't been knocked down. The referee takes eight seconds to assess the boxer's condition and he, not the boxer, determines if the boxer is fit to continue.

> Many of the dysfunctions we see in leaders are due to unprocessed pain.

Admitting that you're hurting does not mean you've lost your faith. God is still good even when the world is bad. It also doesn't mean that you're placing blame. You can acknowledge who is responsible for the sake of adjusting your boundaries, not for growing bitter. Admitting you're hurting is also not about surrendering your power and playing the victim. There is no need to forfeit your future victories. This is simply the time the focus is on you.

Pity is defined as the feeling of sorrow and compassion caused by the suffering and misfortunes of others. If you can have pity on others, why can't you have pity on yourself? In the words of my dear friend, Dr. Jaquet Dumas, "Pretending to be O.K. does not make you O.K."

If you're going to have a pity party, you need to invite the right people. Do not broadcast your pain all over social media. The internet is not your personal diary. Social media followers and friends are not really your friends. When you're in pain, you need compassion and faith, not drama!

Jesus went to the home of Jairus and found paid weepers putting on a dramatic spectacle of grief, and he tossed them out! Instead, he brought in with him three trusted members of his staff. He shut the door and resurrected the little girl.

I'm not saying that if you "only believe" you will receive everything you want or that every dead thing in your life will be resurrected. What I am saying is that as your life is elevating, you may experience painful disappointments. I am reminding you that in those times, God still speaks. He still gives instructions and his word is still good.

When life delivers you a gut punch, don't try to power through. Lean on the right people to catch your breath. Listen for the voice of God and hang on to your hope, your mind, and your memory.

Pace Yourself

You don't need me to tell you that your dream will require work. But you may need me to tell you that it also requires rest. The third way we lose our breath is known as respiratory stress. It happens when a person runs at a high speed for a long distance without breaks. This is most difficult to avoid when you do what you love and you're excited to see your vision come to pass.

What do we want? Vision! When do we want it? NOW! As a Christian, I endeavor to be like God. Sure, I want to be loving, faithful, and full of mercy but, the part of God that I most want to emulate is found in Genesis chapter one. The whole earth was without form and God began to cast vision. "Let there be." As soon as He said it, He saw it and it was good. That's the part I like! (Yes, I am rubbing my hands together, tossing my head back and doing that little take-over-the-world laugh, but in a good way.)

Vision is the most exciting thing on the planet. It gathers it galvanizes, it inspires, it motivates. It is a picture of a better future. When I cast vision to my team I am super-excited! I love bringing them with me to a world of pure imagination. However, the next step, although not my favorite, is also my responsibility. That is setting the pace of how this vision will be carried out.

As your life lifts off, your pace will pick up. There will always be something demanding your attention. You will have to learn not just to master time, but to master energy! Read this carefully, because this is vital. One of the easiest ways to destroy a productive person is to get him to deny his limits and then push him past them. The most convenient time to do this is right after a major victory.

> *King Ahab told Jezebel everything Elijah had done and how Elijah had killed all the prophets with a sword. 2 So Jezebel sent a messenger to Elijah, saying, "May the gods punish me terribly if by this time tomorrow I don't kill you just as you killed those prophets. 3" When Elijah heard this, he was afraid and ran for his life, taking his servant with him. When they came to Beersheba in Judah, Elijah left his servant there. 4 Then Elijah walked for a whole day into the desert. He sat down under a bush and asked to die. "I have had enough, Lord," he prayed. "Let*

me die. I am no better than my ancestors."
1Kings 19:1-4 NCV

The Prophet Elijah was fresh off of a spectacular victory. You should read about it in 1 Kings 18. It involved calling out his enemies, trash-talking them, and fire falling from the sky! Afterward, a wicked queen threatened his life and he took off running. He ran until he couldn't run and then he walked until he couldn't walk. By verse four, he was suicidal. Elijah was winded and he couldn't catch his breath.

"Pace protects you from panic!" ~Pam Ross

When you're winded you're subject to delusion. Elijah felt alone. He felt like a failure. He felt ineffective. None of this was true. He was actually winning. The remedy to this state of mind was almost too simple to believe. Elijah went to sleep. While he slept, God sent an angel to him. Not to bring him a message or plans for his next great victory. The angel brought him lunch! Elijah woke up, ate lunch, and went back to sleep. The angel came back a second time. He brought Elijah more food. This time he also had a message for the prophet. "Get up and eat. If you don't, the journey will be too hard for you."

At the time of this writing, I've walked with God for decades. I can assure you that every promise I have ever received cost more time, extracted energy, and demanded more effort than I ever would have expected. I would do it all again. I have learned to pace myself and trust God to take me where He wanted me to go. I've had to fix my eyes on God, catch His rhythm, and match His pace.

Life will ask a lot from people on the rise. As your success becomes evident, people will want your time and your wisdom. It feels good to finally be in demand. You need to know when to rest, when to eat, and when to sleep. There are times you need to put the whole world on hold and put yourself first.

Flight crews instruct us that if needed, put our oxygen masks on ourselves first. We hear it all the time, but in the moment of emergency, the action would be counterintuitive. This is why you must be deliberate about developing habits of self-care. Let's end this chapter by giving you my top three self-care habits.

Practice Breathing:
Breathing is the fastest cure for anxiety. Breathing is the easiest way to alleviate tension. Breathing is the reason cabins are pressurized. Air at higher altitudes is

under less pressure. The molecules are spread out and harder to inhale. That's why the flight crew must pressurize the plane before takeoff.

Take a few minutes in your day to just sit and breathe. Center yourself and remember who you are and where you're going. Bring things into perspective and remember what is important. This habit will pay off when you're under pressure. This works when I'm faced with a hard question or I have to be patient or I need to overlook an opportunity to be offended. Your next level is dependent upon your responses on this level.

Command your Calendar.

My mom used to say to me "let me know when you have a day off." I would always answer, "Tell me what you need, and I'll schedule it." I've grown to understand that if I don't fill my calendar, someone else will.

Parkinson's law is the adage that "work expands to fill the time available for its completion." It basically suggests that if I give myself two days to complete a project it will take two days. When the same project would have taken me one day if I gave it that amount of time. I don't believe that Parkinson's Law is always true. Some things are just going to take time. However, I do believe that whatever you give your time to will fill it. So, I schedule one day a month that is just for me and do what makes me happy.

Think Long-term

Thinking long-term is key to all of my other self-care habits. My ability to pace myself hinges on long-term thinking. Long-term thinking is why I invest in my mental and physical health. It is also why I budget my financial resources. Remember this, the poorest among us live hour by hour, trying to make it from day to day. The average American lives from month to month. The wealthiest among us live and plan from generation to generation.

Those are my habits. Each of us is wonderfully different. So, put some real thought into who you are and what you need to remain at peace. Practice those things now so that when the unexpected happens and it will happen- you will have a place of peace inside of you. You will never be among those who go from place to place, from placebo to placebo looking for peace. You'll carry it with you.

Life can be uncertain, but how you respond can be very predictable. Good habits train you how to respond to pressure so that when you get to the top of your mountain you will pass the final test. In the face of the unexpected, just keep breathing.

Postscript

Congratulations! You made it to the end of the book. I am so proud of you!! Here is some final wisdom for your amazing journey.

The process described in <u>Get Ready to Fly</u> is an elevation cycle. The final chapter speaks about mastering your responses to the unexpected. As you journey, you will eventually encounter something that provokes a wrong response out of you. It generally feels like one of the following;

"Whoa! Where did that emotion come from?"
 "Did I say that out loud?"
"I thought I was done doing this!"

When pressure squeezes something ugly out of you, you'll be tempted to do one of two things. The first is to ignore it and just keep it moving. (Hey, I only did it one time. It doesn't mean anything.) The second is to be so focused on what you did that condemn yourself. (How could I do that? I am a terrible person.)

Take my advice and avoid these pitfalls. Instead, focus less on what you did and more on why you did it. A negative response to pressure is not an indication of failure. It's an indication of a need to grow. It's time to honestly face your issues and deal with that luggage again. Thus, the cycle of success and elevation begins all over again.

- New levels of Freedom lead to a greater sense of …

- Identity. A greater sense of identity requires stronger…

- Commitment. Stronger commitments will help you control your…

- Appetites. The sharper your disciplines the easier it is to monitor your …

- Communication. Monitoring your communication will guard your …

- Response to the unexpected

As the old song goes, every round goes higher and higher. Happy Flying!

pR

> *Beloved, I pray that you may prosper in all things and be in health, just as your soul prospers. 3John 2*

References

1. The Notorious B.I. G. "Mo Money Mo Problems" Songwriters: Christopher Wallace / Sean Combs / Mason Betha / Bernard Edwards / Steve Jordan / J Phillips / Nile Gregory Rodgers

2. Wikipedia contributors. (2020, February 13). Death of Aaliyah. In Wikipedia, The Free Encyclopedia. Retrieved 20:53, February 15, 2020,from https://en.wikipedia.org/w/index.php?title=Death_of_Aaliyah&oldid=940583727

3. https://www.nytimes.com/2001/09/08/arts/haste-errors-and-a-fallen-star.html

4. https://www.cnn.com/2011/12/06/showbiz/alec-baldwin-flight/index.html

Pam Ross is an Inspirer with a powerful ability to identify and activate the genius in others. She is a multiplier who has led hundreds of teams and thousands of individuals to dramatically increase their personal leadership and team-building ability.

"Our greatest wealth is found in people who find the courage to discover and embrace who they really are."

Pam uses various forms of media to reach a global audience with her dynamic message of serving, leading and loving. She is the author of <u>Serving, Leading and Loving, a survival guide for Kingdom leaders</u>, the <u>Serving, Leading and Loving personal development guide</u>, <u>The Force of Joy, building an unstoppable you</u> and <u>30 Days of Joyful Living</u>. Pam is the host of The Culturalist, conversations with Pam Ross, Podcast.

Pam is the president and lead trainer of Kingdom Leadership Development, a non-profit training and consulting organization. She is also Executive Director of Leadership and Culture at All Nations Worship Assembly, Global Headquarters and The Culturalist for the ANWA Collective. Pam is the mother of three adult daughters, Imani, Nia and Zoe.

Visit <u>PamRoss.com</u> for books and resources by Pam Ross

Made in the USA
Middletown, DE
13 December 2025